D0339065

"In *Parenting Your Parents*, Grant and Tammy Ethridge give voice to the millions of adults who are currently caretakers for their aging parents. With compassionate insight born from personal experience and refreshing wisdom from God's Word, they remind us that caring for our parents is a blessing, not a burden. This book is a must-read for anyone seeking clarity, peace, and encouragement amid this uniquely bittersweet season."

Chris Hodges
Senior Pastor, Church of the Highlands
Author of *The Daniel Dilemma* and *What's Next?*

"As someone who cared for and loved his mom until she died at 104 years old, I can affirm how important Dr. Grant Ethridge's *Parenting Your Parents* will be for so many. Read this to be informed and encouraged!"

Jim Cymbala
Pastor, the Brooklyn Tabernacle
Author of *Fresh Wind, Fresh Fire*

"I believe in Grant and Tammy Ethridge. Their heart for people oozes from this book as they desire so passionately to help each of us on this unique journey of parenting our parents. As a pastor, I will share this tool with so many of our people who are right now walking through this difficult time. *Parenting Your Parents* is biblical in content and current in our culture. Read it and share it with a friend."

Ronnie Floyd
Senior Pastor, Cross Church
President, National Day of Prayer
Past President, Southern Baptist Convention

"Grant and Tammy are a blessing to me and have been faithful stewards of the gospel for years. They serve as remarkable examples of what it means to prioritize the gospel in our families. This book is a helpful resource for those like myself who want to care well for aging parents with the utmost honor and grace for the glory of God."

J.D. Greear
Pastor, the Summit Church
President, Southern Baptist Convention

"Grant and Tammy Ethridge have addressed a universal challenge that Baby Boomers have either experienced recently or are going through now—becoming a parent to our parents. One has to wonder why someone hasn't addressed this before? They do it from firsthand experience, compassion, and a level of candor that makes it truly practical and encouraging."

Mike Huckabee
Former Governor of Arkansas
Host, TBN's *Huckabee*

"Grant and Tammy Ethridge are model parents and have a model marriage. They have both the credibility and the character to teach us how to continue to honor our parents when they need our care the most. I wish I'd had this book when my parents were still living."

James Merritt
Lead Pastor, Cross Pointe Church
Touching Lives Ministries
Past President, Southern Baptist Convention

"This much-needed book from Grant and Tammy Ethridge is not merely theoretical but filled with applicable and practical principles that have been beaten out on the anvil of personal experience. Get it now...before you need it!"

O.S. Hawkins
President and CEO, GuideStone Financial Resources

"I have cared for my parents and in-laws. Now I'm thinking about my children's role in my life. Thanks, Grant, for a book to help me understand my future."

Johnny Hunt
Pastor, First Baptist Church Woodstock
Past President, Southern Baptist Convention

"In their extremely helpful book *Parenting Your Parents*, my dear friends Grant and Tammy Ethridge answer many questions that those of us with aging parents have asked. They also give helpful ideas about getting through this very trying time. This book is a must-read for all of us who find ourselves parenting our parents.

Fred Luter
Pastor, Franklin Avenue Baptist Church
Former President, Southern Baptist Convention

"You never quit parenting—even when your kids are older. Then to your amazement...you find yourself parenting your parents! How do you pull that off? You can begin with Grant and Tammy Ethridge's new book. Grant and Tammy have been there and done that. Practical, powerful, and personable...this book is so good, you will pass it on to others!"

Dennis Swanberg
America's Minister of Encouragement

"As a psychologist who has counseled thousands of families, I can tell you this book is much needed, and I highly recommend it to you!"

Charles S. Lowery
President, Lowery Institute for Excellence

"I am so thankful for *Parenting Your Parents* by Grant and Tammy Ethridge. Having been a pastor for almost three decades, I've walked with many families through this season of life, and I am thrilled to have this amazing new resource to recommend. The authors provide biblical guidance and practical suggestions that help people along on this difficult journey. Grant and Tammy's Christlike compassion for people oozes from every page of this book!"

Vance Pitman
Senior Pastor, Hopechurch

"Get this book! It needs to be on your shelf for the future or to give to a friend in need. Most importantly, you may need to read it thoroughly because caring for your parents is the chapter of life you have entered. Good resources on how to parent our parents are few and far between. Grant and Tammy leverage the transparency of their own lives and godly wisdom to bring hope to our journey. Let them lead you on the path they have walked of loving and caring for their parents well."

Gregg Matte
Pastor, Houston First Baptist Church
Author of *Difference Makers: How to Live a Life of Impact in Purpose*

"This book addresses a common but emotionally difficult dilemma that most of us will face at one time or another. With compassion and practicality, Tammy and Grant Ethridge help us navigate the waters of caring for aging parents. Their writing will support you in your quest to honor your father and mother with insight, compassion, and biblical wisdom. You will find help, relief, and joy in the serving throughout its pages."

Jay Strack
President and Founder, Student Leadership University

"My wife and I are parenting our parents, and I cannot think of a book that would be more helpful for baby boomers in this season of life. Grant and Tammy are two caring, loving, open, and transparent people who share their heart and passion for honoring our parents in this final stage. On top of that, all they share is founded on their faith in Jesus Christ. This book will be a help to so many."

Bryant Wright
Senior Pastor, Johnson Ferry Baptist Church

Parenting
Your
Parents

GRANT AND **TAMMY ETHRIDGE**

HARVEST HOUSE PUBLISHERS
EUGENE, OREGON

Cover design by Studio Gearbox

Cover photos © Yaroslav Danylchenko / Stocksy ; Chinnapong / shutterstock

Italics in quoted Scriptures indicates emphasis added by the authors.

Parenting Your Parents
Copyright © 2019 by Grant Ethridge and Tammy Ethridge
Published by Harvest House Publishers
Eugene, Oregon 97408
www.harvesthousepublishers.com

ISBN 978-0-7369-7722-7 (pbk)
ISBN 978-0-7369-7723-4 (eBook)

Library of Congress Cataloging-in-Publication Data

Names: Ethridge, Grant, author. | Ethridge, Tammy, author.
Title: Parenting your parents / Grant Ethridge and Tammy Ethridge.
Description: Eugene, Oregon : Harvest House Publishers, [2019]
Identifiers: LCCN 2019000527 (print) | LCCN 2019004765 (ebook) | ISBN 9780736977234 (ebook) | ISBN 9780736977227 (pbk.)
Subjects: LCSH: Aging parents—Care—Religious aspects—Christianity. | Adult children of aging parents.
Classification: LCC BV4910.9 (ebook) | LCC BV4910.9 .E84 2019 (print) | DDC 248.4—dc23
LC record available at https://lccn.loc.gov/2019000527

Printed in the United States of America

19 20 21 22 23 24 25 26 27 / BP-AR / 10 9 8 7 6 5 4 3 2 1

Acknowledgments

It takes a winning team to care for parents, and it takes a winning team to put together a project like this book. We want to express our thanks to the excellent team at Harvest House. They have been a joy to work with. We'd also especially like to thank our good friends Ron and Michelle Smith. Without their persistent encouragement we would have never taken on this project. To everyone who assisted and contributed in any way, from conception to completion, thank you.

"Miss" Tammy is the love of my life and my best friend. She's been by my side faithfully every step of the way in our 34 years of marriage. God has blessed us with five children and eight grandchildren, and our story is a God story. It's been an incredible ride! Tammy, I can't wait to write the next chapter of our lives with you. Every day I wake up knowing the best is yet to come.

To our parents, siblings, children, grandchildren, and extended family, thank you for loving us through the good times and not so good times. Through it all, we *are* family, and we love you. To our moms' sisters, thank you for faithfully calling and checking on our mothers. Their days are always brightened when you do, and your kindness means so much to us.

Stephanie Fortune has been my assistant for more than 12 years. She's become like family to us, and Tammy and I don't know what we'd do without her. Few people have the professionalism, dedication, and heart for ministry Stephanie does. Without her careful attention to detail and every written word, this project would not have been completed. Thank you, Stephanie. We love you!

It's a joy to be the senior pastor of Libertylive.church in Hampton

Roads, Virginia. This community of faith demonstrates what it means to be part of God's family and to live out the gospel. I also want to thank our mothers' churches in Georgia. The relationships they enjoy there have stood the test of time. Thank you for all you do to minister to them.

Ultimately, we thank our Lord and Savior Jesus Christ, who is our Shepherd. Apart from Him, we can do nothing. With Him, we can do all things.

Contents

The Journey Begins...

Maybe it's just the season of life we're all in, but it seems as if everyone we talk to who's our age is caring for a parent. We cared for our own dads in their last days, although long distance. Caring for them was challenging with so many miles between us, but what a joy it was to be by their side at the end of their lives. And as they lay on their death beds, we reassured them we would take care of our moms.

Tammy and I love our mothers, but we couldn't know what the future would bring. We couldn't know what that commitment would look like. With my mother, it started with the grief process and concerns about her living alone. Then it progressed to back surgery; rehab; medications; falling at home alone; a brain bleed; emergency surgery; rehab again; falling again; a broken hip; selling the business, the autos, and the home place; and finally moving her from Georgia to Virginia to live close to my brother and me. There was no way for us to know ahead of time how hard all that would be on us all—physically and emotionally.

At the same time, Tammy and I were trying to help her mother through cancer (a double mastectomy and chemo treatments), knee surgery, heart surgery, and a host of other issues.

Caring for parents should be a privilege, not a burden. After all, they cared for us when we couldn't care for ourselves, and it's natural to want to be there for them. Having been a pastor for more than 35 years, I had watched many others travel down this road, but I still had no clue what the journey would be like until I walked a mile in their shoes. And *wanting* to be there and being *able* to be there are different.

It's our prayer that in this book you'll find practical tips from those who, like us, have been there, encouragement as you face complex decisions, and comfort as you walk the road ahead.

Tammy's Take: This season has been one of the most challenging and difficult in my life. The shift from being the child who's parented to parenting parents has definite pitfalls, and it's easy to get stuck. Both my mom and I have been challenged—her not wanting to be told what to do by her little girl and me trying to help without being bossy. It's a slippery slope to navigate. I definitely needed someone to say, "This helped me," or "That was a disaster; don't do or say that!"

Grant and I discovered that few books or resources on the subject of parenting your parents exist (although in this book we've quoted from a number that do). Our prayer is that this book will give other families an additional resource of encouragement for this journey—a resource we wish we'd had. We are the sandwich generation, caring for our aging parents while also supporting children who are in college, paying for weddings, and enjoying our grandchildren. (I knew we'd entered a new phase of life when I witnessed my mother-in-law on her walker and my granddaughter in her walker collide head-on.)

This book is our story. It's what we wish we'd known before we started this season, and we hope you'll find yourself laughing and crying but most of all believing you can make it with God's help. After all, family has been His plan from the beginning. We need one another. Life was never intended to be lived alone; we were made to do life together. That's why the Bible has so many commands to love one another, pray for one another, prefer one another, forgive one another, encourage one another, and comfort one another. So, from our family to yours, let's do this—for one another.

1

You Are Not Alone

The Lord is my shepherd; I shall not want.
PSALM 23:1

One study estimates that a fourth of all adult children are providing personal care or financial assistance to a parent.[1] *One in four.* While that statistic is surprisingly high, if you're caring for a parent, you can find comfort in knowing you're not alone.

As I mentioned in the introduction to this book, Tammy and I have been there. As a pastor and pastor's wife, we've also talked to many others as they've moved through this hard season, often unprepared, filled with more questions than answers, sometimes while still raising their own children.

As you learned if you ever brought a newborn child into your home, people don't come with instruction manuals. Even if they did, how much good would that do? Every child is different. The same is true of our parents and us because every parent and every child is unique. What you'll face in caring for your parents and the feelings you'll experience will be uniquely yours. Yet, in the big picture, you won't be alone.

> *What you'll face in caring for your parents and the feelings you'll experience will be uniquely yours.*

A 2015 study by AARP revealed that 34.2 million adults in the

United States had been a caregiver to an adult 50 years or older in the prior 12 months.[2] Another resource says that at least a third of all family caregivers care from afar.[3] This tells us that many people not currently in the position of caregiver are likely to be one day.

The Lord Is My Shepherd

Arguably, because it's the best-known and most-loved psalm, the Twenty-Third Psalm has brought more peace and comfort to the masses than any other passage of Scripture. We can all use a little peace, comfort, and guidance as we deal with the daily task of caring for someone else—especially when that someone else is a parent. Throughout this book we'll walk through this psalm together, applying it to the situations you'll face—not to provide cookie-cutter answers but so you can personally encounter the Great Shepherd right where you are.

Over the years, many sermons and books have influenced my commentary on the Twenty-Third Psalm. Jerry Vines, James Merritt, Tony Evans, Phillip Keller, and others have given me fresh insight on the passage. I'm grateful for their influence on my life, and I pray that just as their words have been a blessing to me, the words you read on these pages will be a blessing to you.

Psalm 23:1 says, "The Lord is my shepherd; I shall not want." Jesus tells us time and time again that He provides for those who follow Him. Everyone is following someone. Who is your shepherd?

You Are Not Alone

A fourth of all adult children are providing personal care or financial assistance to a parent.

As many as 34.2 million adults in the United States are caregivers to an adult 50 years or older.

A third of all family caregivers care from afar.

I Shall Not Want

If the Lord Jesus is your Shepherd, you have everything you need. But that doesn't mean you have everything you want. The Bible doesn't teach a prosperity gospel—that everyone who follows the Lord will be rich and have whatever they desire. It also doesn't teach a poverty gospel—that if you want to follow Jesus, you have to sell everything you own and have nothing. We have a providential gospel: The Lord is everything we need and more.

While Psalm 23 is often read at funerals, it's about all the days of your life, including right now. You might be a single mom or dad, a senior adult, a college student, or a widowed person saying, "I don't know how I'm going to make it." But if the Lord is your Shepherd, He will meet your needs. No problem or need will come your way that He can't handle.

> *If the Lord Jesus is your Shepherd, you have everything you need.*

David wrote Psalm 23, and the shepherd boy who became king also said, "I have been young and now am old; yet I have not seen the righteous forsaken" (Psalm 37:25).

Tammy and I don't know what your specific situation is. We don't know what your bank account looks like or what personalities, living situations, health issues, and life experiences factor into your position. But we do know that if Jesus is your Shepherd, you'll never lack what you need. Even in the midst of caring for your parent and the unique issues you face, you are not alone.

2

Put On Your Own
Oxygen Mask First

He makes me to lie down in green pastures;
He leads me beside the still waters. He restores my soul.
PSALM 23:2-3

Tammy and I fly often, and we have more crazy airport stories than anyone I know. One of the funniest is from a family trip to Grand Cayman. The church we served in Arkansas for almost 20 years sent us there for our 15-year anniversary at the church.

We had never been to the Caribbean, and in Arkansas, the closest we ever got to the ocean was in Gulf Shores, Alabama. But as we looked forward to our trip, we decided to take diving equipment, and we packed it all into one hard-shell suitcase. Have you ever noticed that the same stuff you packed *going* won't fit on your way back? As we packed to return home, this suitcase was so full that the whole family had to sit on it to get it closed. Then I put a travel strap around it for extra support.

When we arrived at the airport, a lady at security asked me to put the suitcase up on the table because she wanted to open it and search it by hand. I don't know why I said this (clearly, I wasn't thinking), but I guess I was so relaxed that it just came out: "When you open this one, it's going to explode!"

I could tell by the look on her face that I was in *big* trouble. I had to clear up the misunderstanding—immediately!

Tammy's Take: As Grant tried to recover from the situation he'd just caused, I stood with our four children, watching and listening. Then, throwing his arms in the air, these unforgettable words came from Grant's lips: "No! That is not what I meant! I was trying to say that when you open this suitcase, it's going to go boom!"

Our oldest son said to me, "He's an idiot!" Grant admits that, at that moment, he could not have agreed more. ⸏

Somehow, we managed to get out of the airport with no handcuffs, arrests, or casualties, and our family laughs about this incident to this day.

Since then we've learned to not cram so much into a suitcase, but unfortunately, sometimes we still pack too much into our schedules. That can cause an explosion that wreaks havoc on our physical and emotional health, our family, and those around us.

Because we fly so much, I've learned all sorts of ways to fly well. For example, I can tell you what to do in case of an emergency. The nearest exit might be behind you instead of in front of you, so locate it before the plane takes off. Remember that your seat cushion becomes a flotation device in case of a water landing (unless a flotation device is under your seat instead). Learn how to put on an oxygen mask when it drops down from above after a loss of cabin pressure.

And don't forget to secure your own oxygen mask before helping anyone else with theirs.

Securing your own mask first might seem completely unnatural, especially if you're a parent, but research has proven that it's vitally important. Destin Sandlin, an engineer known for his YouTube educational series called "Smarter Every Day," partnered with NASA scientists to test the reasoning behind this instruction. He took part in a training where astronauts learn the effects of hypoxia (oxygen deficiency) on their bodies.

Sandlin went into a specialized chamber and removed his oxygen mask. It took only a few minutes for shapes to become unrecognizable and for him to not be able to secure his oxygen mask without help from someone else. This test was done at 25,000 feet, but he points out that most airplanes fly at around 35,000 feet, where there is much less oxygen. That means Sandlin's minutes of useful consciousness during the test would have been only seconds in real life.[1] And it means if you don't secure your own oxygen mask first on a plane, if instead you help someone else secure theirs (like a child's), it might be too late for you to secure your mask at all.

While not all safety and security guidelines given on airplanes are practical for life, a great deal of insight is behind the directive to put on your own mask first, especially when caring for others.

Tammy's Take: Grant and I have to remind each other of these guidelines from time to time. Not trying to cram so much into our lives and taking care of ourselves is the only way we'll survive this journey of parenting our parents.

You'd probably be willing to admit that caring for someone else can be stressful. You might also admit that it can make you tired, irritable, or just plain grumpy. In Virginia Morris's book *How to Care for Aging Parents*, she says caregiving can make people physically sick, and that it actually increases mortality rates.[2]

Other research on the health impacts of caregiving yields comparable results. A study by MetLife shows that "adult children 50+ who work and provide care to a parent are more likely to have fair or poor health than those who do not provide care to their parents."[3] When we focus so much on the needs of others, it can be easy to forgo our own regular medical tests and checkups. We can also tend to eat unhealthily and get fewer hours of sleep.

In their book *Caring for Your Parents*, Hugh Delehanty and Elinor Ginzler reveal that "women who care for ill parents are twice as likely to suffer from depression and anxiety as noncaregivers. They have higher levels of stress, hostility, and self-criticism than the general public."[4]

So what is one to do with this information? Put on your own oxygen mask first. Take care of your own health so you'll be healthy enough to assist your parent. Have you had a physical recently? Maybe you cringe at the thought, but heed this recommendation from Carolyn Hartley and Peter Wong in their book *The Caregiver's Toolbox*: "Get a baseline physical exam at the earliest caregiving stages so that you can track your own health." They go on to say that "every physician, every caregiver book, and every elder care attorney will remind you that you must take care of yourself."[5]

In addition to sacrificing their own health, many caregivers sacrifice time they would have otherwise spent with their own children or grandchildren. "Caregivers of aging parents often find themselves 'sandwiched' between assisting two generations and face difficult, stress-inducing decisions about how to allocate resources."[6] As MetLife explains, they have less money and time to help their own children with what's important to them. They also have less time for leisure and personal tasks. Such sacrifices are hard enough, but when they go unnoticed or unrecognized by a loved one, caregivers can also feel unappreciated.

Worse, some caregivers feel guilty and ashamed if they care for themselves first, believing that means they're inadequately providing care for their parent. As Barry Jacobs states in his book *The Emotional Survival Guide for Caregivers*, "It is neither necessary nor helpful to feel ashamed."[7]

Tammy's Take: I've felt this shame. When my dad died several years ago, I wanted to help my mom and take care of her. But we lived eight hours away, so I thought it made perfect sense to move her close to me. The problem was she wasn't ready for that move. She wanted to stay in her own home, attend her own church, and be close to friends and family in her familiar place. (I get that. It would be a heart-wrenching, difficult decision to make.)

Over time, we have had to come to the understanding that if she can't move here, neither can I spend a lot of time there. I'm committed to my husband, family, and church. I'll go to her when I can and in emergency situations, but frequent or extended visits aren't an option for me right now.

You can't force an adult parent to do what you want, but at the same time, they can't be offended or hurt if you're unable to put aside everything else in your life—spouse, children, grandchildren, a job. There's only so much of you to go around. I have to lay that shame at the feet of Jesus and ask Him to work in me—and in her—to accomplish His purposes. ⬦

If Destin Sandlin taught us anything, it's that you must put on your own oxygen mask first. We'll soon be unproductive and ineffective in helping others if we don't. "Numerous studies show that the caregivers who offer the best care to their parents are the ones who take care of themselves and take advantage of available help and support."[8]

An email I received while preparing for this book began, "My story started when I was 31. I already had my hands full with a 12-year-old and 4-year-old..."

This woman had two kids, an unsupportive spouse, and a father diagnosed with lung cancer. She ended her email

> *Superman and Wonder Woman don't exist in the real world.*

with this realization: "I can't be Wonder Woman." No one can. Superman and Wonder Woman don't exist in the real world.

Everyone needs rest, time for themselves, and time with the Lord. God the Father rested after creation. Genesis 2:2 says, "On the seventh day God ended His work which He had done, and He rested on the seventh day from all His work which He had done." Not only did God rest, but He made remembering the Sabbath one of the Ten Commandments:

> Remember the Sabbath day by keeping it holy. Six days
> you shall labor and do all your work, but the seventh day

is a sabbath to the LORD your God. On it you shall not do
any work...For in six days the LORD made the heavens and

> *Everyone needs
> rest, time for
> themselves, and
> time with the Lord.*

the earth, the sea, and all that is in
them, but he rested on the seventh
day. Therefore the LORD blessed
the Sabbath day and made it holy.
(Exodus 20:8-11 NIV)

And in the New Testament, we read
that Jesus Himself got away to pray (Luke 5:16). It's not selfish or weak
to rest or take time to be alone with the Lord. It's biblical.

He Makes Me to Lie Down in Green Pastures

Continuing our look through Psalm 23, verse 2 says, "He makes
me to lie down in green pastures." You are insufficient, but our Great
Shepherd is all-sufficiency. He will ensure you never lack for green pastures. Think about what a green pasture is to a sheep—not just a place
to graze but a place to snooze. It's a place of rest. There's nothing like a
good meal and a good mattress!

Are you sick and tired? Sometimes you just have to go home and
lie down. Most of us don't like to do that when we feel responsible for
getting things done. But God gives His beloved rest, and sometimes
He makes sure we lie down.

> *You are insufficient,
> but God is
> all-sufficiency.*

I know I might be a little weird, but
I like to iron clothes, and I won't let
Tammy iron my shirts. I want to do it.
I once worked in a men's clothing store,
and ironing is just something I enjoy.
The way to get your clothes looking best is to apply steam or heat. If
you want that collar to lie flat and the wrinkles pressed out, ironing is
what you do. Think about your hair. Have you ever had a bad hair day?

Had a wild hair sticking straight up? How do you get it to lie down? Put hot water on it and apply pressure!

Sometimes God will let you get into some hot water, allowing the trials of life to apply pressure to make you lie down. For sheep, wool grows most during the quiet times, and we need to remember that when we're resting, God is working.

Are you feeling the pressure of caring for your parent? The Great Shepherd wants to give you rest! Lie down in His strong arms.

Or at least sit down. Before Jesus fed the five thousand, He didn't have them lie down, but He did have them sit down. If you want God (or in a lot of cases *need* Him) to multiply what you have (your time, your strength, your wisdom), you must at least sit down. You must be still for God to do His best. Psalm 46:10 says, "Be still, and know that I am God."

Practical Ways to Get Help

Kid swap—Take turns with a friend watching each other's children. You won't have to pay for a sitter, and your kids can spend time with their friends.

Meal swap—Take turns with a friend cooking dinner for each other's families. Even not cooking one night a week can free up a little time to relax.

Hire a sitter—Pay someone you trust to sit with your parent or your children one day a week.

Enroll your parent in an activity—If your parent enjoys an activity, look for opportunities for them. Drop them off for an hour at an exercise or craft class. They'll have fun, and you can read a book or go for a walk while they're there.

Online shop—Have your groceries or other items you need delivered to your door or order them ready for pick up at the store. Use the time you save to relax.

He Leads Me Beside Still Waters

God even gives us opportunities to be still.

If sheep fall into rough or deep water, they can easily drown because their wool absorbs a lot of liquid. For us, life has many storms, sending us into turbulent waters. Thank God for *still* waters!

> *The Shepherd takes full responsibility for the well-being of His sheep.*

In caring for your parent, if any troubled waters are of your own making, ask God for forgiveness. Ask your loved one for forgiveness. Then move on. Accept it, learn from it, and be still. Don't make the same mistake again. If you're in troubled waters not of your own making, ask God to calm the stormy situation and give you peace.

And if God leads you to still waters, thank Him!

He Restores My Soul

The beginning of Psalm 23:3 says, "He restores my soul." The word *restore* means "to bring back." The Shepherd takes full responsibility for the well-being of His sheep. Did you once have energy, patience, joy, and a good relationship with your parent? The Lord can restore those things. Are you stressed, lonely, or weary? Too tired to pray? Isaiah 40:31 tells us, "Those who wait on the LORD shall renew their strength."

But is the Lord your Shepherd? Nothing in this psalm applies to you unless you have a relationship with Him. Maybe you used to spend time with God, but you haven't talked to Him lately. Now is the time. Whatever you want, whatever you lack right now, tell the Shepherd. If you're tired, let Him restore your soul.

It might be hard to believe, or seem not very practical, but the Lord can and will give you everything you need amid the medical bills, insurance questions, doctors' appointments, and hectic schedule. He can show you practical ways to rest, to get away, and to spend time with Him. He will provide opportunities. Walk in them.

Practical Ways to Help Yourself Unwind

Read a book.

Go for a walk or exercise.

Watch a movie.

Visit the beach or a park.

Get a massage.

Attend a sporting event.

Take a bike ride.

Enjoy a bubble bath.

Spend time with good friends.

While doing all of these might not be practical, plan and schedule (as in block the time on your calendar) at least one activity a week. Make your own rest a priority.

Stay healthy and social. Find quiet moments every day to spend time with the Lord and to be honest with Him about what you're feeling. Go to bed early. Take a day to sleep in, and don't feel guilty about it. Just as I packed too much into one suitcase, maybe you need to stop packing so much into your schedule. If you don't control your calendar, everyone else will. If you try to be everything to everyone, you won't be anything to anyone. Don't neglect yourself. Don't neglect your spouse and your children.

Look to the future. To be hopeful is to look forward to something. What are you looking forward to? What is your spouse looking forward to? What are your kids looking forward to? If you can't answer those questions, you might be out of touch and trying to do too much.

———————

Remember, you have to put on your own oxygen mask first. You must be able to breathe. It's essential to establish this before it's too late.

3

Honor

He leads me in the paths of righteousness for His name's sake.
PSALM 23:3

Have you heard this story about the 80-year-old couple? They were having a hard time remembering things, so their doctor encouraged them to write what they needed to remember on a sticky note and then place it where they would be sure to see it.

That night, as they were watching television, the husband got up to go to the kitchen. The wife asked him to bring her a bowl of ice cream. She also suggested that he write down her request so he wouldn't forget what she wanted.

"I've got it," he said. "You want a bowl of ice cream."

"Yes, but I want strawberries on top. You should write that down so you don't forget."

He assured her he understood and repeated the order to her.

"Yes, but I want whipped cream on top of my strawberries," she said. "You'd better write that down or you're going to forget."

The husband, agitated at this point, repeated everything to her again and then left the room.

Thirty minutes later, he came out of the kitchen and handed his wife a plate of bacon and eggs. She stared at it for a moment, and then she looked at him and said, "I told you. You needed to write it down. You forgot my toast!"

This story is so funny to me. While it's meant to be comical and give you a laugh when I'm sure you could use one, it also reminds us of some of the issues we face as our parents get older. Whether they just need to use sticky notes or require advanced care, challenges are inevitable. They arise whether or not we're ready, and they arise in all shapes and sizes. No matter the issue, one reality is the same: Our role as their children must change.

Once when our kids were small, we were driving down the road with my mom in the front seat. The car in front of me stopped quickly, and I had to slam on the brakes. As I did, I reached my arm out across my mom to protect her. In that moment, I realized my role was changing. A similar occurrence happened when my father-in-law was riding with me a few years later.

You know in your heart when the shift has occurred. You begin caring for your parent, and that can be a hard change because it can feel so unnatural. This is a difficult transition for you both. Change in any form is often hard, but your parent, someone you once saw as so strong, now looks to you for help and support, even for simple things. Sometimes the change happens suddenly and sometimes more gradually, over time. Either way, now you're responsible for caring for your parent.

> *Our parents are not our children. They never will be.*

Still, our parents are not our children. They never will be. This is so important to remember. We must navigate through these deep waters with grace, understanding, patience, forgiveness, love, and strength from the Lord.

While the toll this role reversal takes might be great, and the stress of it can wear us thin, the Bible is clear that we are to honor our parents—always. This command was given originally in the Old Testament as part of the Ten Commandments (Exodus 20:12), and then it was restated in Ephesians 6:2: "'Honor your father and mother,' which is the first commandment with promise." We are to obey our parents when we're children, but the Bible says that when we marry, we leave our parents and unite with our spouse (Genesis 2:24). So while we still listen to our parents as adults, we don't always obey them.

Never is there a time, however, when we should cease to honor them. Ephesians 6:2 says this commandment has promise—great blessing in honoring our father and mother.

Before we go further, let's be honest. For some of you, the idea of honoring your parent might cause your stomach to churn a little. Maybe your mother is completely undeserving. Maybe your father has hurt you so badly that you don't see how you could possibly show him honor.

Or maybe you resent your parent for putting you in the position you're in. Life has become much harder than you ever thought it would be, and somehow you see that as their fault. You find yourself blaming them even though you know they have no control over this.

Maybe you even resent God for where you are. You believe He should have prevented your situation. You pray and pray but don't see results.

Your feelings are real and common. May I take a moment to pray for you before we go further?

Father, thank You for my friends reading this book. Simply because they have read this far, I know they have a desire to better care for their parent. You see the exact circumstances they're in and know the exact feelings they're feeling. You know if bitterness or resentment is present. I pray that You will soften their hearts toward You and toward their parents.

Father, please help them to be open to help and wisdom. Through the power of Your Holy Spirit, enable them to love their parents, forgive their parents, and honor their parents in the days ahead. Please show them how to do that, not in their own strength but through the strength You give. Thank You for Your love and forgiveness. Thank You for seeing and caring

*about the situations we face. Please encourage my friends now.
In Jesus's name, amen.*

Be encouraged. The Bible says, "With God all things are possible" (Matthew 19:26 NIV). Let's trust in that promise as we move ahead.

Practically speaking, what does it mean to honor your parents? *Honor* as a verb means "to hold in honor or high respect" or "to treat with honor." As a noun, it means "honesty, fairness, or integrity in one's beliefs and actions."[1]

> *With God all things are possible (Matthew 19:26 NIV).*

Honoring your parents means to respect them, treat them fairly, be honest with them, and treat them with dignity. It means not talking down to them. It's hurtful and degrading for them to be reprimanded or to be talked to as if they don't understand. Honoring them depends on you, not on them. No matter what they do on their end, you're responsible for honoring them on your end.

A more specific way you can honor your parents is by encouraging their independence. Virginia Morris suggests that instead of completely taking over their household chores or finances, let them do as much as possible. Instead of being condescending to them about what they can't do, affirm and validate what they can do. Independence is good for both their physical and emotional well-being. "Your parent may welcome your help but...when they no longer make their own decisions, when they are treated as needy and helpless, they grow only more needy and more helpless. As they give up increasing amounts of control, they also give up their self-esteem, spirit, and drive. They wither."[2]

Honor your parents by celebrating and appreciating their gifts and abilities and encouraging them to keep at them. Someday you might have to step in for safety reasons, but even then, do your best to foster independence in the areas you can.

In addition to fostering independence, you can include parents in decision making, especially in decisions involving them. It's never too

Practical Ways to Foster Independence

Social events—Help your parent regularly attend a book club, a senior fitness class, a church group—someplace that's their own.

Household tasks—Let your parent make the grocery list, check the mail, or do their own laundry or cooking.

Recreation—Encourage your parent to do crafts, play games, work puzzles, walk with a friend—some activity they would enjoy.

Input—Let your parent make decisions about what gifts they will give, where they'd like to shop, what hobbies they'd like to pursue.

Connection—Encourage your parent's relationships with other family members and friends.

Everyone's situation and abilities are different. Check with your parent's doctor to make sure activities they want to participate in are safe for them.

early to start talking about the future. You can begin with hypothetical situations, saying something like, "Mom, if something ever happens to Dad, what would you like to do?" or "If you ever get sick like Miss Louise is, how would you like to be cared for?" The most important thing is to begin the conversation and keep it going. You'll hear me say this again and again throughout this book: Even if decisions are made, situations might change. Leave room for adjustments, and listen to what your parent is saying. Everyone likes to be heard.

Tammy's Take: My dad was talking to my mom, Grant, and me a few days before he died. He said if my mom passed before he did, he would sell the house and come live with us. Looking back, knowing that was unlikely to happen, I believe he was telling us what he wanted her to do upon his death. Regardless of his intentions, I determined in my heart and mind that my mother should do exactly that when he died.

With that thought in the forefront of my mind, I began thinking and planning in that direction for her without considering her feelings or wishes in the matter. I thought I was honoring what Dad wanted for her, but I was dishonoring her and her feelings. She had spent a lifetime building sweet memories with her husband and children in that house—too many to just casually walk away from them just because that's what I wanted. If she sold the house and left right then, in her deepest time of grief, it would be harder for her to remember and relive all the amazing times she'd had in that place.

She had familiarity there, a home there, a life there. She had friends and family. She knew where to find the grocery store, pharmacy, church, bank, hospital, and her doctors' offices. Whatever she wanted or needed, she could quickly and easily access it. And I was asking her to abandon it all. If she moved to our city, everything would be new, getting around would be difficult, and all her memories would be bundled up in a few boxes and tucked away.

In my mind, I was going to help her, take care of her, build new memories with her, and spend more time with her. I could justify moving her closer to me in every way, but that was really about me, not her. She was still active—driving, cooking, cleaning, shopping, taking care of herself and even others in her family, church, and community. What I was really doing was asking her (telling her) to give up everything *for me*. This was not honor, not love, and not care. This was pure selfishness, even if unintentionally so.

One day my mom might need to sell her home and come live with us. If and when that happens, God will give her the grace to do what needs to be done. Until then, my job is to love and honor her, asking our heavenly Father to watch over her and protect her, using her in this season of her life for His glory—just where He planted her so many years ago.

When including your parents in decision making, work with them to prepare any important legal documents that will ensure their wishes are honored. They need to have an updated will and power of attorney, and an advance directive or living will, where they can indicate what type of medical care they would like if they are unable to communicate. (These documents will also help you significantly when faced with end-of-life decisions.)

If you know the Lord, one of the greatest ways you can honor your parent is to lead them to Him. Jesus is the greatest gift you could ever give anyone. Sharing Him with your parent might be the greatest honor you ever have.

If your parent or parents already know the Lord, encourage them in spiritual things. The Holy Spirit can do more than you could ever do.

Honoring a parent can take many forms. If you're in a situation where your parent or circumstance has made it difficult for you to do so, ask the Lord how you might honor your mom or dad. He knows them, and He knows you. He knows everything that's been said and

> *Honoring our parents doesn't require promises.*

everything that's been done. He knows the emotions involved. He'll show you how you can honor them even in the messiest of situations.

Here are a few cautions. While we often want to please our parents, don't make promises you might not be able to keep. Honoring our parents doesn't require promises. Sometimes a parent asks us to commit to something now that might not come up for years. It's so easy to say, "Yes, I promise." We love our parents and would do anything for them.

However, we don't know what the future holds. We don't know what our finances will be or how circumstances might change. If you make a promise and then you're not able to fulfill it, even because of something beyond your control, you might feel guilt or extreme disappointment—or like a failure—in addition to experiencing your grief over losing them. A better response when a promise is asked is "I'll try" or "I'll see what I can do when that time comes."

Honoring a parent also doesn't mean you have to do everything they say or ask. For instance, as we noted earlier, it's important for you to take care of yourself and your family. To do that, you might have to set boundaries with your parent or say no. Parents might even try to manipulate their children or use guilt tactics to control them. But you can make your own decisions and still honor your parent.

He Leads Me in the Paths of Righteousness for His Name's Sake

The second half of Psalm 23:3 says, "He leads me in the paths of righteousness for His name's sake." This is the second time the word *leads* is in this psalm. We have to make all sorts of decisions when caring for our parents, ranging from where they'll live to what medical care is best to how much help they need with daily tasks. Rest assured that no matter the decision you're facing, the Lord will lead you. When trying to honor your parent, He will lead you. When trying to help your parent, He will lead you.

> *You can make your own decisions and still honor your parent.*

Maybe you've made some wrong choices along the way, or maybe you never thought you'd end up where you are now. I encourage you to seek the Lord on what is the right path for you and your family. Seek Him on how to honor your parents as you care for them. Proverbs 14:12 says, "There is a way that seems right to a man, but its end is the way of death." When left to our own decisions, we might choose wrong. However, Psalm 37:23 says, "The steps of a good man are ordered by the LORD, and He delights in his way." When we let the Lord order our steps, He will make them firm.

You might be thinking, *How do I get on the right path?* or *How do I listen to God on topics like which doctor is best?* I'm glad you asked.

The first way is through God's Word. Psalm 119:105 says, "Your word is a lamp to my feet and a light to my path." While a specific doctor's name isn't given in Scripture, the Bible speaks to all of life's situations. The Word is alive and active and is relevant to where you are today.

Another way is through the Holy Spirit. If you're a Christian, the Holy Spirit indwells you and will lead and guide you if you let Him. John 16:13 tells you that the Spirit will "guide you into all truth."

I also encourage you to seek godly counsel. Proverbs 1:5 says, "A wise man will hear and increase in learning, and a man of understanding will attain wise counsel." Proverbs 12:15 says, "The way of a fool is right in his own eyes, but he who heeds counsel is wise." Talk to those who have cared for their parents or who are professionals in the field. Listen to people you trust and to those who are wise, giving you God-honoring advice.

Sheep have poor vision. They can easily take the wrong path. They have to listen to the voice of a shepherd. Sometimes you make wrong choices when you listen to the wrong voices. Well-meaning family members and friends might be leading you down the wrong path. God is our Shepherd, and He will lead us in the right direction if we listen to Him. God sees the future. He sees what you and I cannot see ahead. As Corrie ten Boom said, "Never be afraid to trust an unknown future to a known God!"

When asked about caring for her mom, one lady in our church said, "I wish I would have prayed more about my mom's care and asked others to pray with me about everything concerning it and the decisions I made." Don't let this be you. Start involving the Lord in your decisions.

Psalm 32:8 says, "I will instruct you and teach you in the way you should go; I will guide you with My eye." James 1:5 says, "If any of you lacks wisdom, let him ask of God, who gives to all liberally and without reproach, and it will be given to him." Isaiah 30:21 says, "Your ears shall hear a word behind you, saying, 'This is the way, walk in it.'"

Seek God's guidance daily. Scripture promises over and over that He will lead us.

God's glory is the ultimate goal. He leads us in paths that are right for His glory, for His name's sake. Think back on your life. Remember the hard times and how God brought you through. Reflect on His faithfulness. He's still that same God! He will be faithful to you in this season, just as He was before.

Tammy and I taught on caring for parents at our church one night, the last night of a parenting series. It was a great series, and we had a lot of fun with it, but that last night was hard. Tammy told our congregation that taking care of parents is more difficult than taking care of babies, toddlers, or teenagers. Through tears, she explained a little about the road we were walking and how our emotions were so raw. Your parents are your *parents*. Nobody else is what they are to you, nor will they ever be. You've known your parents longer than anyone else, you've loved them longer than anyone else, and they've loved and supported you longer than anyone else.

> *Build a bridge with your parent that will carry you into the days ahead—with no regrets.*

In this season, you can't fix their hurt or heal their disease. You can't turn back the clock and return to the way things were. But you can be there to love them through the days ahead. You can support them while so much is changing for you both, and you can help them adjust. You can honor them as you walk this path together.

Tammy's Take: It might be that you, like me, have tried to force your parent to do something that only drove a hurtful wedge into your relationship. This is not how we want to remember our last years together. Humbly ask God to forgive you and lead and guide you in helping your parent. Then humbly go to your mom or dad and ask for forgiveness, reassuring them of your love and restoring the honor that God asks us to give. This can build a bridge with your parent that will carry you into the days ahead—with no regrets.

4

Help—Part One

Yea, though I walk through the valley of the shadow of death,
I will fear no evil; for You are with me;
Your rod and Your staff, they comfort me.

PSALM 23:4

Help! That's probably what you were thinking when you picked up this book. And if you're like me, you grew up watching your parents care for their parents.

My parents cared for my dad's parents first and then my mom's parents. But they lived next door to each other. Their yards met. It was ingrained in me that parents took care of us when we could not take care of ourselves, and we should do the same for them.

First Timothy 5:8 says, "If anyone does not provide for his own, and especially for those of his household, he has denied the faith and is worse than an unbeliever." Galatians 6:2 says, "Bear one another's burdens, and so fulfill the law of Christ." Caring for our parents is certainly biblical, but it's not always simple.

Since we've been married, Tammy and I have never lived close to our parents. Our society has become much more mobile than it used it be. People are also living longer today. My grandfather's dad died in his fifties, but my grandfather died in his eighties. Because of advances in medical care, people no longer need just a sponge bath; they may need an IV or other complex medical care or treatments, even while still at home.

The next two chapters provide you with ten practical ideas from people who have been there and who have great advice to share. While caring for parents isn't simple, it is doable. You can make it through. You can even come out on the other side with sweet memories to cherish.

Yea, Though I Walk Through the Valley of the Shadow of Death...

Before we get into some specific helps, let's draw some more encouragement from Psalm 23. Verse 4 begins, "Yea, though I walk through the valley of the shadow of death." God balances life with green pastures, still waters, valleys, and mountaintop experiences. We are often okay with God leading us to green pastures, still waters, and in the paths of righteousness, but valleys? *No, Lord!*

> **No, Lord!** *should never be an answer when God leads us.*

No, Lord! should never be an answer when God leads us. Why doubt Him now? God is a good Shepherd.

Life has some real valleys. Sometimes you're in a valley with mountain walls so high they block the sun, causing a shadow. You can't see anything, and the mountain walls squeezing in on each side are causing you to feel trapped, lonely, and hopeless. Those are dark times.

Notice the word *walk* in verse 4. Keep on walking. Don't quit. Keep going. If you fall, get up and keep walking. If you have a long way to go, keep walking. Even though you'll experience many turns and twists on the way and it's dark, keep walking until the morning comes. Psalm 30:5 says, "Weeping may endure for a night, but joy comes in the morning."

Also notice the word *through*. Some things you're going through with your parent or family might not make sense, and you don't understand them. You feel as if this valley will never end, or that you'll never laugh or enjoy life again. Take heart. This valley did not come to stay;

it came to pass! It might get worse before it gets better but keep walking. Don't give up hope. God will keep you safe, standing, stable, sane, and strong if you rely on Him.

Valleys have an entrance and an exit. Why would a shepherd lead his sheep into a valley filled with danger and death threats? To get to a better place. If this season of caring for your parent is a valley for you, keep it all in perspective. God is taking you to greener pastures. He's leading you to still waters. Sometimes He has to lead you through the valley to get you where you need to

> *Keep on walking. Don't quit. Keep going. If you fall, get up and keep walking.*

be. Don't mistake the process for the purpose. The process is temporary; the purpose is eternal. The only way *out* is *through*, and we can do all things *through* Christ (Philippians 4:13).

The next part of verse 4 says, "I will fear no evil; for you are with me." Notice that David moves from using *he* to *you*. He's said the Lord makes, leads, and restores him, but now instead of talking *about* God, he's talking *to* God. The valleys of life draw us closer to God. We're more prone to talk *about* God in green pastures and still waters, but we cry out *to* God in the valleys. Life-and-death situations cause us to cry out to God in desperation.

Are you desperate today? Cry out to Him! The presence of Christ in our darkest times gives us boldness and confidence. You'll get through this because He is with you.

> *You'll get through this because He is with you.*

The last part of the verse says, "Your rod and Your staff, they comfort me." A rod is for protection, and a staff is for correction. God has a rod in one hand to fight off anything that threatens you. He has a staff in His other hand to pull you out when you get stuck and to draw you close to Him. Notice the verse doesn't say He'll take you out of the valley but that He'll comfort you through it.

1. Plan Together

Tammy was hosting a baby shower at our house not too long ago. I heard her tell another woman who was helping that they needed to come up with a plan. She said, "Let's execute the plan before it executes us!" Plans are so important. You wouldn't start building a house without drafting plans. Coaches come up with game plans, entrepreneurs come up with business plans, and we constantly evaluate our retirement plans. Plans help us prepare for what's ahead so we can achieve our desired outcome when the time comes.

Why is it so hard to plan ahead when it comes to caregiving? Just as we would plan for a business or to build a house, we should plan for the future when it comes to our parents. Death is inevitable for everyone, right? "Talking about the worst-case scenarios won't make them come true, and refusing to talk about them won't make them go away. Ignoring the inevitable will only leave you unprepared for a crisis that is sure to come."[1]

Many people don't think about the what-ifs. More times than not, a great deal of anxiety surfaces when children think about their parents being unable to care for themselves, so they just push aside the thought, hoping they won't find themselves in that position.

> *Just as we would plan for a business or to build a house, we should plan for the future when it comes to our parents.*

They also don't discuss plans among family members. Talking can bring up topics that are hard, sensitive, and personal. And it's a risk because wedges that already exist can be driven further and further into relationships. But talking can also be an opportunity for families to grow closer to God and to one another, and thoughtful planning can help avoid emotional turmoil and the pressure that comes with time-sensitive decisions.

Planning together is the first tip I put after the "Honor" chapter. As Tammy and I have already said, including parents in discussions is an important part of honoring them. If they're still able to have rational and realistic conversations, their opinions should be heard. After all, you're talking about *their* life and *their* care. You would want the same done for you.

It's also important to include your siblings in these conversations (most of us have siblings). "In the long run, the discussion will go better if it happens before a crisis forces everyone to make decisions on the fly. Without that pressure, family members can work to ensure that everyone's fears and anxieties are addressed, and that no one feels demeaned, diminished, or excluded."[2] If your brother needs more time to process all the possibilities, he has it. If your sister lives out of state, you have time to schedule a face-to-face meeting where the discussion can be more personal and meaningful.

> *Thoughtful planning can help avoid emotional turmoil and the pressure that comes with time-sensitive decisions.*

You might learn that your brother is planning to be much more help than you thought, or that your sister-in-law has been down this road and has a great deal of wisdom and compassion to share. You might learn that this challenge can bring you closer together.

Maybe you've found yourself wondering where to even begin. That's okay. It's normal to feel overwhelmed or even a little scared before having such a conversation. I have great news for you: "God has not given us a spirit of fear, but of power and of love and of a sound mind" (2 Timothy 1:7). Isaiah 41:13 says, "I, the LORD your God, will hold your right hand, saying to you, 'Fear not, I will help you.'" The Lord will be right there with you. Fear is not of Him. "Perfect love," which Jesus is and has for you, "casts out fear" (1 John 4:18).

A good place to begin is to consider the most common changes that can occur as people age; they often show up in any research on aging. Their bones and muscles weaken, so they lose strength and might be less coordinated. This also means they're more susceptible to injury and pain in their muscles and joints. Their brains aren't as sharp as they once were. It might take longer to learn or remember things, and they might become forgetful.

Their eyes and ears also weaken. Their hearing and sight might need more attention. As people age, gastrointestinal problems can increase, creating a need for a healthier diet and planned exercise.

Anticipating these changes prompts us to think carefully about them and prepare for them.

Tammy's Take: I found reading those last paragraphs depressing. Wow. Look at what we have to look forward to—bones and muscles weakening, poor coordination, injury, pain, confusion, forgetfulness, vision and hearing problems, GI problems...(It all sounds so *glamorous*, doesn't it?) Realizing what we could have ahead of us, though, let's take care of our physical bodies now.

As Christians, our bodies are the temples of the Holy Spirit, and we need to be the best we can be for as long as we can. I've seen young people who've abused their bodies quickly grow old and people who've taken care of their bodies remain active even into old age. For the sake of our parents, spouses, and children who might have to take care of us, for the glory of God and to remain active in His kingdom as long as He gives us on earth, let's take care of our temples, which are ultimately His temples.

With this encouragement from Miss Tammy in mind, let's dig deeper into ways we can plan for the changes that occur as people age. One way to prepare for these changes is to simply ask questions. What-if questions are great because what-if scenarios aren't certain, and that's a good thing. So are open-ended questions, with no necessarily right or wrong answer. We can discuss them without feeling pressure or emotional strife. We can casually ask our parents about medical care, living situations, and finances, and we can ask our siblings about their care preferences or assumptions if something were to happen to Mom or Dad.

Even with a plan in place, sometimes tough decisions have to be made, and there's no clear right or wrong. Agree with your siblings to discuss what's happening with one another, but also decide what you'll do if no consensus can be reached. The important thing is to get everyone's wheels turning and the lines of communication open. Then, when you *need* to talk later, you've already begun. The doors are already open within the family.

It's also possible that your parent will be the one who's not ready for these conversations, and in her book *A Bittersweet Season*, Jane Gross gives us some good advice:

> *The important thing is to get everyone's wheels turning and the lines of communication open.*

> Note whether your parent's attitude to your first overture is "resistant," "reluctant," or "ready." If it's resistant, prepare for the fact that it might take several tries. If it's reluctant, proceed gently, look for openings, and encourage any expression of willingness to review current and changing circumstances. If it's ready, let your parent guide the conversation because it means he's already been thinking about it and has just been waiting for you to give him this chance.[3]

The important thing is to plan, sooner than later, and to do it together, with both parents and all siblings if possible. Your mom and dad might have the ability to make decisions and express wishes now that they won't have later.

Just as you do with a financial plan, house plan, or business plan, write down or type out what you've decided. Record your caregiving plan. Putting words on paper takes your plan from an idea to reality. Include as many details as possible about what you, your parent, and

Five What-If Questions to Ask Your Parent

1. What if someday you find that you can't manage your finances? Who would you like to help you?

2. What if your health deteriorates and you can't live at home? What would you look for in a new place to live?

3. What if you start needing more help in the future? Would you be willing to move closer so we can take care of you? If not, what would your preference be for care?

4. What if you become so sick that you can't make health decisions on your own? What are your quality-of-life/end-of-life preferences?

5. What if you need more care than I can provide? What is your preference beyond me/our family?

Remember not to make promises you might not be able to keep.

your siblings agreed to. While it might feel weird to distribute that record, make sure everyone has a copy. Explain that you want everyone to know what you talked about so that if you all ever need to refer to it, everyone will be in the loop. Make your plan clear and understandable, and update it as needed.

> *Putting pen to paper takes your plan from an idea to reality.*

Dwight D. Eisenhower, a prominent army general and the thirty-fourth president of the United States, is known for saying, "In preparing for battle I have always found that plans are useless, but planning is indispensable." Bill Belichick, head coach of the New England Patriots, referenced this quote when asked about the importance of planning and preparation before the 2015 AFC Championship Game.

He went on to say that when the game happens, most times you have to adjust.[4]

There's no way to know everything now about the care your parent will need. Plan as best you can, but come up with a plan B and maybe even a plan C. When the time comes, you might not be able to follow the first plan. You might have personal situations that keep you from it.

> *Blessed are the flexible, for they will not be bent out of shape.*

Finances might change, and health challenges can pose unforeseen circumstances. You have to be flexible and, again, keep the communication lines open. I love the quote that says, "Blessed are the flexible, for they will not be bent out of shape."

When plans have been drafted together, the hope is for buy-in from everyone. And when adjustments need to be made, everyone can pitch in. If someone isn't supportive, at least they'll know what's happening and won't be in the dark if something goes wrong. Planning together, and being willing to adjust along the way, will certainly help you in the days ahead.

2. Get Organized and Stay Organized

"A critical aid to survival is getting organized early on. As experienced caretakers will confirm, the initial up-front effort will go a long way toward relieving the stresses of caregiving down the road."[5]

You can take steps now that will help you be efficient as you move forward. No one likes to waste time or to feel as if things are spinning out of control. Getting organized now will keep you from frantically searching for what you need later.

After you've begun the conversation with your parent and your siblings about your parent's care, start preparing. You'll need certain documents, papers, and pieces of information no matter what. You can get organized before you're faced with an urgent situation.

Do Your Parents Have an Estate Plan?

If your parent does not yet have a will or a trust, encourage them to get one. If your parent has a will, do you know where it is? You'll need the original document, not just a copy. Copies won't always suffice in court. When was the will last updated? Sometimes people save old documents that have since been revised. You'll need to access your parent's most recent will in the event of their death.

Determine if your parent needs a trust. You don't have to be wealthy to need one, and many people find them helpful. While a will says, "When I pass, this is what I want to happen with what I own," it's still a limited document. A trust, on the other hand, appoints a trustee to watch over and manage what people leave to their beneficiaries. A will is a public document, but a trust is private. If you don't want people to know the details of your personal business, you need a trust. Many people will choose to have their will state that all their possessions go to the trust. That way, matters can be handled privately. Both revocable and irrevocable trust options are available, with different advantages for each.

> *While your parent is still in good health and able to make sound decisions, encourage working on an estate plan.*

Creating these documents honors a parent's wishes and helps them plan ahead. While your parent is still in good health and able to make sound decisions, encourage working on an estate plan.

Throughout Scripture, we see stories of those who are faithful in passing a legacy from one generation to the next. So for all of us, how we handle our estate reflects what we value. A will or trust says, "I spent my life accumulating these possessions, and this is how I want them to be used."

At Libertylive.church, where I serve as senior pastor, we have the Liberty Legacy Endowment. Your church or denomination might have something similar. These endowments are opportunities to help ensure that certain ministries continue, well beyond your lifetime. Consider a trust that settles outstanding bills and then gives

90 percent of the remainder of your estate to your children and 10 percent to your church.

Do Your Parents Have a Power of Attorney?

A durable power of attorney is a legal document that gives another person authority to make decisions if you're unable to do so. Various documents exist for your parent to consider. For example, a general power of attorney gives broad authority on legal and financial matters, while a health care power of attorney grants authority for making medical decisions. Both are important. If your parent doesn't have these in place, help them get this done. These documents simply say, "If something happens to me, here's the person I want to handle my financial or medical decisions." Some people designate one friend or relative in their health care power of attorney and another in their financial power of attorney.

Estate plans, wills, trusts, and power of attorney documents enable parents to proactively make their wishes known ahead of time.

If your parent does have these documents in place, make sure you know where they are. Different states require different processes (papers witnessed, notarized, and so on) and different wording on their durability, so check with an attorney you trust—in the state where your parent resides—to learn what your parent will need.

Do Your Parents Have a Living Will?

While living wills are often tied with health care power of attorneys, they're different. A living will has advance directives on the type of medical care you would like to receive if you're unable to make those decisions. The living will specifies one's desires when it comes to things like resuscitation and other end-of-life/quality-of-life decisions. It's important for all adults to have a living will (even you!) because no one knows when a crisis might occur.

Estate plans, wills, trusts, and power of attorney documents enable parents to proactively make their wishes known ahead of time. They also allow decisions to be made about their care while emotions are at a minimum.

Tammy's Take: A living will confirms what medical interventions you desire in the event that you're unable to verbalize them. As my dad neared death, my parents, Grant, and I discussed what we wanted the end of his life to look like. My mom, who wasn't having any medical issues at the time, said she didn't want any lifesaving measures at all, not even an IV. My dad, knowing that his time was short, quickly said, "Well, I think I want an IV! What if I get thirsty?"

This is a perfect example of how emotions are affected by our circumstances. I had heard him say many times before that he didn't want anything prolonging his life into more pain and misery, but once he was close to death, he began to question himself.

A living will doesn't mandate withholding comfort measures, but it clearly states what your parent does not want. Once again, talk with and *listen* to your parents' wishes, giving them honor during their last days and moments of life.

Elder care attorneys specialize in these services. If you need any help, talk with one. They'll often offer one free consultation, and then you can decide if you'd like to proceed. They can help with estate planning, medical directive documents, wills, trusts, financial planning, and more. Keep in mind that laws vary from state to state, so it's important to meet with an attorney from your parent's state of residence.

Do You Have Access to Your Parents' Medical Information?

Compile a list of a parent's doctors and pharmacists, along with their contact information. Include a medical history and current prescriptions, along with allergies and past surgeries. You can even keep extra copies printed so they'll be easy to provide if you go to a new doctor's office. Copies of the insurance card(s) are helpful as well.

Because of HIPAA laws, privacy is a priority for medical offices. If your parent is okay with it, they need to list you as someone who can access their records. This will need to be done at each practice. You can explain that you aren't trying to take over or be nosy, but it will help with even simple needs, such as being able to pick up a prescription.

Do You Have Access to Your Parents' Password-Protected Accounts and Locked Items?

Do you have keys to your parents' house, car, safety deposit or post office box? Do you know the combination to their safe? Think about what you might need to access, even accounts with cell phone and cable companies. Ask, "Where do you keep your passwords and PINs, just in case I need them?" While a parent might not be comfortable giving up keys and codes right away, keep at it. Even if just one of the adult children has access, that person can become a resource when needed.

Do You Know Where Your Parents Keep Important Papers and Cards?

You might find yourself needing your parents' driver's licenses, Social Security or Medicare cards, insurance policies, titles to vehicles, deeds to property, federal and state tax returns, and outstanding bills. Make sure you know where these items are in case you need to access them.

Are You Prepared to Take Notes?

According to AARP, "You must become a note-taking dynamo, keeping track of daily appointments, medication schedules, phone numbers, to-do lists, and other bits and pieces of information...Taking notes on conversations with doctors and other caregivers, with dates attached."[6]

You might find using your smartphone works best for you, or

perhaps a notebook or folder. Whatever it is, just keep this information together. Sticky notes stuck in random places around the house are not recommended. When you need to make an important phone call, you shouldn't have to search high and low for the phone number you need.

———

If you and your parents don't live in the same town, make a list of what you need to get done while you're visiting them. Do more than just socialize; set aside time for important preparation. Plan ahead and execute that plan.

Organizing information might not happen quickly. These are personal items and personal information your parent might not be ready to hand over. Make a list of what you don't have but *need* to have.

> *Keep everything in one place so you can quickly find what you need.*

Over time, work with your parent to get these things together. You don't have to get them all at once. Don't try to take over. You're not asking them to give you complete control; you simply want to be knowledgeable about their whereabouts so you can help if ever needed. But compile what you learn and what you gather. Use a notebook, a filing system, a computer file—whatever works best for you. Keep everything in one place so you can quickly find what you need.

Organization helps lower stress. Tammy and I know we can be much more productive and think much more clearly in a clean space. The same is true when it comes to caring for your parents. Keep information and items relating to their care in order. Don't let clutter and chaos add to your stress.

3. Access Available Resources

It is estimated that "eighty-five percent of all caregivers do not know how to be a caregiver."[7] Most people who care for their parents have had no training or knowledge about what to do. If you have no idea where to start or have way more questions than answers, take heart. Help is available.

A parent's doctor (or that doctor's support staff) is a wonderful place to start. A good doctor knows your parent and the exact conditions and obstacles Mom or Dad is facing. What's more, most doctors are familiar with the health challenges people face as they age. If you've found a doctor you and your parent (or parents) trust, you have a wonderful source of expertise and assurance.

> *"Eighty-five percent of all caregivers do not know how to be a caregiver."*

While doctors might not have extended time to work with you, they can often direct you to specific resources you can turn to for information and support. For example, if your parent has been diagnosed with Alzheimer's or dementia, your doctor should be able to direct you to organizations that specialize in facing these challenges. Such organizations provide reliable information, referrals to support groups, helpful tips, online resources, and more. And if you don't think one doctor is enough help, seek a second opinion or contact your local area agency on aging or a local senior center.

Tammy and I also encourage you to talk to those who have been there. When you're open about what you're facing, you might find that one of your friends is a few steps ahead of you on the road. You can learn from their research and experience and what or who has been most helpful to them.

If you're looking for more information on a certain topic, do a Google search. However, be careful about what you read. Make sure the sites are credible. Is the information supported by research? What are the credentials of the people providing advice? By the way, I caution against reading the discussion boards or opinion threads on websites; they often feature questionable advice from people who aren't professionals in the realm of elder care.

The main point here is that all kinds of helps are out there; you just need to look for them. Are you concerned about a parent's driving capabilities? AARP, AAA, and your local Department of Motor Vehicles all offer resources. Do you want your parent to have more social interaction or exercise? Talk to your local YMCA, church, or community center.

> *Remember, you are not alone. You don't have to navigate these waters by yourself and without a map.*

You don't have to navigate these waters by yourself or without a map. Don't be afraid to ask for help or do research. You'll save a lot of time and heartache learning from others.

4. Assemble a Support Team

Comedian Milton Berle once said, "Laughter is an instant vacation." It's so true! When you laugh, you get a short break from life's harsh realities. What makes you laugh? Is it YouTube videos, comedians, certain friends, or family members? My wife, Tammy, as well as my kids and grandkids, do it for me.

For example, my oldest son, Taylor, and I were talking at the Southern Baptist Convention Annual Meeting a couple of years ago. This a national meeting the majority of pastors in our denomination attend. Taylor was in the middle of telling me something when O.S. Hawkins walked by. (Hawkins is president of GuideStone, the company that manages my retirement plan.) I immediately turned away from Taylor and started talking to Dr. Hawkins. When I eventually returned my attention to my son, he said, "Dad, that was so rude! I was in the middle of talking to you, and you just walked away."

I said, "Taylor, you don't know who that man is. That's O.S. Hawkins, the man in charge of my retirement." Without missing a beat, Taylor said, "Dad, you don't know who I am. I'm the man in charge of your retirement *home*!"

While they might not even know it, my wife, my kids, and my

grandkids are part of my support team. They're in my corner and help me when I need it, even if it's just with a laugh.

When it comes to caregiving, we all need people in our corner. We need people who are on our team, fighting for the same goal. Ecclesiastes 4:9-12 says,

> Two are better than one, because they have a good reward for their labor. For if they fall, one will lift up his companion. But woe to him who is alone when he falls, for he has no one to help him up. Again, if two lie down together, they will keep warm; but how can one be warm alone? Though one may be overpowered by another, two can withstand him. And a threefold cord is not quickly broken.

In 2015, The National Alliance for Caregiving (NAC) and the AARP Public Policy Institute commissioned a study that resulted in some eye-opening statistics on caregivers. The report says that the average duration of caregiving is four years, but 24 percent of caregivers provide care for five years or more. Twelve percent provide care for ten years or more.[8] Also, "on average, caregivers spend 24.4 hours per week providing care. About 1 in 4 provide care for 41 hours or more each week."[9] That's a significant amount of time, especially if you're still parenting your own children and/or working a full-time job.

When it comes to caregiving, we all need people in our corner.

As our children grow, they need less help. However, as our parents age, the care they need increases. This thought can be frustrating and overwhelming, and we have to remember that this is just a season. Our kids were small for only a season, and we'll need to provide care for our parents for only a season. But when you begin taking care of your parent, you don't know how long that season will last. While you might be able to handle what's needed on your own initially, you won't be able to keep it up long-term. Assembling others to help is crucial.

As Tammy and I will say repeatedly in this book, you cannot care for your parent alone. Assembling a support team is crucial for your own health and to provide the quality care and assistance your parent needs.

Who are the people on your support team? Who is available to help you? In some cases, when less care is needed, it might just be your spouse or siblings. In other cases, you might have a social worker, a home health nurse, and an elder care attorney on your team.

Begin by evaluating where you are. Make a list of people currently helping you and what they're doing—even include how often they're helping. What takes up the most time? Which tasks are the most difficult? The goal is to determine not only what's currently being done but to think through what needs to be added or adjusted.

If you have trouble accepting help, ask yourself the following questions from Barry Jacobs's book *The Emotional Survival Guide for Caregivers*. Is it:

- "Because you feel caregiving is a privilege?

- Because no one else can do the job as well as you?

- Because in your judgment, you have more time and energy for the task than anyone else?

- Because it would feel like shirking your responsibility, which would make you feel guilty?

- Because you made a commitment, and making any change would feel like breaking it?

- Because you've begun to define yourself solely as a caregiver?"[10]

It's okay to ask for help. Asking for help is healthy. That's why we encourage it so strongly.

Jacobs also asks, "What will really make you feel supported?" He adds, "Your fondest wish may be to have someone split the practical caregiving tasks with you. But perhaps having someone to talk to at the end of the day would lighten the load even more. Or maybe an aide with limited nursing skills has a bedside manner that makes everyone in the family feel so at ease that you're all willing and able to pitch in more on the practical necessities. When support is concerned, the important factor in deciding what to accept is whether it's really any help to you."[11]

Asking for help is healthy.

What do you need?

Family meetings can help put a support team in place. While the term *family meeting* might have a negative connotation (I can almost hear you groaning now), they can be productive and helpful in the long run. I suggest starting with just the immediate family. You may need to include others later, but initially keep the attendance small unless someone else is playing a significant role in caregiving. Before you meet:

- *Be in prayer over the meeting.* The Holy Spirit can do way more than any person ever could. Pray for clear communication, understanding, and clarity on decisions that need to be made. If anyone is resistant or difficult, pray that they will be open and receptive. Pray for unity in the family. Pray for schedules to open for a meeting time to be set. Pray about anything that's concerning you.

- *Schedule a time that works for everyone.* Ideally, everyone will be able to attend the meeting in person. If being in the same physical location isn't possible, try a video call so everyone can be seen and included. It might help to plan something more relaxing or fun along with the meeting. For those able to make it in person, schedule a casual dinner beforehand or some other activity your family enjoys. This will help break the ice and encourage bonding before the more serious discussion begins. Just don't start the conversation too late in the evening. You don't want everyone to be tired before you even start.

- *If you're the family member facilitating this meeting, make an agenda and share it ahead of time.* No one likes to be blindsided. Send out the agenda, saying something like, "While I know we won't be able to solve everything when we get together, here's what I think we need to start with. Let me know if you think of anything else." Make it clear that you want to include everyone's questions and concerns. The topics on the agenda should be there to analyze what needs to be done and then determine who's going to help get it done. The following sample meeting agenda and some suggested guidelines are taken from *How to Care for Aging Parents* by Virginia Morris.

  - **Family Meeting Agenda**[12]
    - What are your parent's current health problems and her physical and cognitive limitations?
    - What are her current needs, in terms of day-to-day help and care?
    - Are there ways to rearrange and renovate her house to allow her to do more for herself?
    - What services are needed in her home or from the community?
    - Is her current living situation working out, or should she move? What options are available?
    - What is her financial situation? Can she pay her bills? Can she afford the services she needs? Is she eligible for, or nearing eligibility for, Medicaid?
    - What, exactly, needs to be done at this point? Make a detailed list.
    - Which tasks can each person take on? Make a list of assignments.

- What might be enjoyable for your parent? (Your parent might *need* someone to deliver meals, but she might *enjoy* visits from grandchildren, daily walks, books on tape, etc.) Who can do some of this?

- Beyond helping your parent, how will each person help and support the primary caregiver?

- What care, services, housing, and financial assistance might your parent need in the future? Is there anything that can be done now to prepare? Who might help with this?

- When will you meet or communicate next?

- Finally, create a plan, in writing, detailing schedules and assignments, and make copies for each person.

- At the end, each person might talk briefly about his feelings about all this, any fears, resentment, grief, etc. (This can be helpful and supportive in a family that is relatively close, but if there are tensions, keep this brief and avoid delving into conflicts.)

- **Suggested Guidelines**[13]

  - No one is allowed to dominate the meeting...use a timer, if necessary.

  - When someone is speaking, others must listen without interrupting.

  - Each person should use sentences that begin with "I"—speaking only about his own opinions, feelings, and actions—and avoid finger-pointing statements that begin with "you."

  - Since your parent's care is the reason for this meeting, all discussions should relate directly to this subject. Steer away from old arguments and debates.

- If your family dynamic is strained, family members are resistant, or the issues are too complex, enlisting the help of an outside facilitator may be best. Ask a social worker, a pastor, or another person not directly connected with the situation who's good at mediating and respected by your family. If you aren't careful, family meetings can spin out of control quickly. As my friend Ron says, "People are often willing to spill their thoughts while they aren't willing to clean up the mess." If you think this may happen in your family, enlist help before you begin.

After the "What needs to be done?" question is answered in the meeting, answering "Who is responsible for what?" will help assemble your support team. Perhaps your siblings are willing to contribute, or, at least, they're giving suggestions for who might be able to help with outstanding tasks. Because not everyone might be local, some of these helpers could be from local senior centers, neighbors, or close friends living nearby. Enlist the help of people you and your parent trust and have all of their contact information readily available.

> *"People are often willing to spill their thoughts while they aren't willing to clean up the mess."*

Teamwork is powerful! Have you seen this acrostic?

T — Together
E — Everyone
A — Accomplishes
M — More

Don't be afraid or ashamed to ask for help. You could be robbing someone of the blessing of helping, all the while exhausting yourself trying to do it all alone. Also, don't be shy about showing appreciation and gratitude. Regularly thank those who support you. No one grows tired of being appreciated!

What will your first step be in assembling your support team?

5. Take Practical Steps

A lady in our congregation emailed me with the top two things she wished she would have known before caring for her mom. First, she wished she would have known more about the Department of Veteran's Affairs' financial benefits. Second, she wished she would have known more about dementia and Alzheimer's so she could have better handled it when her mom acted ugly toward her.

> *You could be robbing someone of the blessing of helping, all the while exhausting yourself trying to do it all alone.*

These are specific; not every person will need to know about VA benefits or dementia, but they will need to know about finances and any specific health issue or disease their parent has. We'll talk about finances and health issues, but first let's cover some everyday precautions that can ensure your parent's safety and your sanity.

Daily Safety

As our parents age, everyday tasks can become more difficult—and dangerous. "Bad eyesight, arthritis, poor balance, multiple medications, and other health problems all put your parent at risk for accidents."[14] It's recommended that you make an assessment. "Spend a day with him observing how he goes about his basic chores...Does he have trouble holding his razor, walking down stairs, heating up spaghetti, or locking the front door? Does he have a [safe] way to get groceries or visit a friend?"[15]

Ask the Lord to open your eyes while you're with your parent in the home and reveal anything that might need to change. As we've said, maintaining your parent's independence for as long as possible is beneficial both to you and to them. Making your mother's home a safer environment will enable her to live there longer. Knowing the risks have been minimized for your dad will enable you to rest at ease.

After you've spent a day with your parent and evaluated their daily tasks, assess whether or not you feel comfortable making the changes that will improve their safety. You can always enlist the help of a professional, such as an occupational therapist or a certified aging-in-place specialist, to point out areas of concern. "Your local Area Agency on Aging may provide referrals for home evaluations within your community, often free of charge."[16] A variety of helpful resources, tips, and videos can also be found online.

Remove anything that could be a fall risk, like throw rugs, electrical wires, and décor in walkways. Add handrails in bathrooms or hallways if needed. Make sure flooring, including carpet, is smooth and level. My brother purchased an emergency call necklace for our mom. She wears it around her neck, and if something happens, she can push the button for help.

Virginia Morris makes these other home safety suggestions:

- designating one button on the phone for 911
- alerting the police and fire departments that your parent lives alone
- making sure chemicals, paints, and medicines are all clearly labeled
- checking smoke and carbon monoxide detectors
- checking for easy escape routes in case of fire
- buying a small, easy-to-use fire extinguisher
- placing specific medical instructions where medics or emergency crews would see them
- having extra flashlights in case of a power outage
- checking outlets and kitchen burners

- adjusting the hot water heater temperature so it cannot burn

- turning up the heat to avoid space heaters and electric blankets[17]

For added security, she also suggests you can install a peep hole and/or an alarm system, make sure your parent uses the door locks, and install outside motion lights.[18]

No matter what steps are needed to make your parent's living situation safer, I encourage you to take them, and to include your parent along the way. Don't just think about what needs to be done or say you'll get to these precautions "one day." Do them. You won't regret it.

> *Don't just think about what needs to be done or say you'll get to these precautions "one day." Do them.*

Finances

"About one in five caregivers report experiencing financial strain as a result of providing care,"[19] and "six out of ten caregivers say that the out-of-pocket costs make it difficult for them to pay for their own basic necessities."[20] Finances are tricky. They're private and are often a sensitive topic. However, money and talking about money are necessary when providing care.

Two aspects to finances are at play: (1) your personal finances and (2) your parent's finances. The statistics above show just how hard caregiving can be on your own finances. For this reason, it's especially important to develop a financial plan.

The MetLife study we've cited before says,

> Caregiving responsibilities may have a dramatic economic impact on both men and women through lost wages due to either reduced hours worked or leaving the labor force early and diminished Social Security benefits or private pensions. Prior studies have presented a range of estimates

Parenting Your Parents

for the impact on lost wages and pension benefits from
$303,260 to $659,139 over caregivers' retirement years.[21]

> *"About one in five caregivers report experiencing financial strain as a result of providing care."*

Budgeting is crucial. It's also advisable to meet with a financial planner you trust to ensure you're making the wisest decisions possible.

Your parent and you might have totally different views on saving and spending, what's expensive and what's not, and what's a need versus a want. As best you can, keep the communication open about finances. Often, it's best for them to meet with a professional as well to make a financial plan. A greater level of comfort might be gained talking with someone who's outside of the immediate situation. You might suggest going together to meet with someone. You can let your parent know you've been thinking of meeting with a professional and offer to set up an appointment for him at the same time.

Let your parent make as many decisions about their money as possible. Gently guide where needed. Again, you would want to make your own decisions if you were in their shoes.

If the time has come for you to manage your parent's finances, you'll need to take these few steps. In *The Caregiver's Toolbox*, Hartley and Wong make these suggestions:

Locate your mom or dad's financial accounts. Credit reports can be helpful in determining what forms of credit your parent has open. Then obtain access to those accounts. A power of attorney will most likely be necessary at this point. After obtaining access, make sure that the accounts have legitimate and current beneficiary and secondary account holders. This might sound simple, but not having these in place can cause additional and unnecessary complications later. They also recommend using technology to manage the process.[22]

While you know your parent best, and she might prefer to see a handwritten, balanced checkbook, it can be helpful for you to manage finances electronically. You can categorize spending, budget, check balances, and so on all with the click of a button.

"When medical bills exceed 5 percent of income, consumers are twice as likely to have trouble making ends meet. Pulling out a credit card to pay for the hospital or physician fees is not the answer."[23] We need to take steps now to be good stewards of all that God has given us. It's much better to plan ahead than to end up in financial trouble later.

> *It's much better to plan ahead than to end up in financial trouble later.*

One other suggestion for finances is to learn how to read and understand medical bills. Hartley and Wong report that "between 45 and 100 percent of the time, your medical bills are inaccurate."[24] Their book also says,

> The Medical Billing Advocates of America, Consumer Reports, Elderweb, and Medical Bill Rehab indicate that the current error rate is between 70 and 85 percent and even up to 90 percent for the elderly. Stephen Parente, professor of health finance at the University of Minnesota, said in a *Wall Street Journal* article that he estimates that errors might be between 30 and 40 percent...Even if the ratio of incorrect codes is one to three, these numbers can be pretty alarming.[25]

When you know what you're looking at, you're better able to tell if the charges are correct. The task might seem daunting, but understanding might save you a lot financially.

Research

Everyone's situation with their parent is different (we'll talk more about this later), so it's important to do what you can to educate yourself on your parent's condition. Has your parent been diagnosed with a particular disease? If so, what do you know about that disease? What do you want to know? "Experienced caregivers tell us that the diagnosis doesn't just happen to the patient."[26] In other words, it happens to the family as well. Don't stay in the dark or on an island alone. If your parent's doctor provided you with information, read it. Again, be cautious about random internet searches; not all information you read will be accurate. Ask your doctor for some trusted websites if you want to learn more.

Researching your parent's condition will help you know what to expect and do if certain events occur. Knowing what could happen in advance will both help prepare you for when it does happen and help you take other practical steps that might be unique for you.

Support groups are available for certain diseases. You and/or your parent might find one of these helpful. Talking with someone who's walking the same road, or who's already been down the same road, can go a long way.

Daily safety, finances, and research are valuable areas to begin, but they certainly don't represent everything to be done. Spend some time considering what would still be helpful or what you know needs to be done in caring for your parent. Make a to-do list. You don't have to check everything off at once, but the list will provide you goals.

Would it be helpful to hold a garage sale to get rid of some items in your mother's home she no longer wants? Add that to the list. Do you want to take your father to see a family member who lives out of state while he's still able? Add that to the list. Add anything you think needs to be done or that would be helpful. Taking these steps along the way and checking them off the list will give you a sense of accomplishment and help you feel less overwhelmed.

How do you eat an elephant? One bite at a time, right?

5

Help—Part Two

You prepare a table before me in the presence of my enemies;
You anoint my head with oil;
My cup runs over.
PSALM 23:5

Now that we're halfway through the ten helps, let's push pause and pick up our look at Psalm 23. These words, written thousands of years ago by David, still bring hope today. The journey of caring for parents can be scary and unknown, but we find hope when we realize God is with us.

You Prepare a Table Before Me in the Presence of My Enemies...

In the first four verses of Psalm 23, we see Jesus as the Good Shepherd. Now we see Him as the Great Host. He has made a room for us to lie down and prepared a table for us to eat. He can put out a spread like no one else.

God made a table for the Israelites in the desert for 40 years. He served them manna, their daily bread. The table of showbread was in both the tabernacle and the temple. Jesus is the Bread of Life.

My grandfather left the old home place to my mom and our family. This was the house my dad's mother grew up in and my mother's dad lived in—at separate times. My mother was born in that house. But my brother and I both live in Virginia and will probably never live in Georgia, so we sold it to the family who lives there now.

I couldn't move the kitchen, but I could move the kitchen table my grandfather made with his own hands. His children, grandchildren, and great-grandchildren all sat around that table. Now his great-great-grandchildren get to sit at it. If only that table could talk! Oh, the stories it could tell.

What happens at the table? Prayer, nourishment, conversation, storytelling, laughter, encouragement, fellowship, and connection. In her book *The Table Experience,* Devi Titus says, "If home is where our hearts are formed, then the table is where our hearts are connected."[1] The table is where we sit face-to-face and talk for at least 30 minutes to an hour. Families might face enemies at school or work, but they can go home to a meal around the table and find love, acceptance, and safety. The table is also a place of education; we learn table manners.

> *The Lord has prepared a table before you now. Will you join Him and draw from Him what you need?*

It's a place of restoration and reconciliation; the prodigal son came home, and his father said, "Let's eat and celebrate!"

The Lord has prepared a table before you now. Will you join Him and draw from Him what you need?

This table is set in the presence of enemies. *An enemy is anything that threatens you.* Even in troubled times, God can set a good table. Even in a bad economy or amid family drama, God can prepare a meal that's good. What's threatening you now? God invites you to step away and commune with Him.

The next part of verse 5 says, "You anoint my head with oil." Insects drive sheep crazy. When flies or gnats get near their heads, the sheep beat their heads against the ground and they won't eat. Do you ever feel as if you're beating your head against a wall? Have you lost your appetite? God won't let the irritations of life drive you crazy. The shepherd's anointing of oil will kill the larva, stop the itch, soothe the pain, and bring healing. The Lord anoints those who are His with the oil of gladness, a repellent against depression and discouragement.

I heard Adrian Rogers, one of our favorite preachers, say, "Anointing is a special touch for a specific task." *Christ* means "anointed one." If Christ is in you, the anointing is in you. *When you have Jesus, you're anointed to accomplish your assignment!*

The last part of verse 5 says, "My cup runs over." In this case, David's cup is running over in the valley, not on the mountaintop. What does "runs over" mean? It means more than enough, like a cup with its contents spilling over the sides. You might feel like your cup is empty and you have nothing left to give. You've been drained by your parent, your siblings, your own family, your situation.

> *When you have Jesus, you're anointed to accomplish your assignment!*

But if you connect to the Shepherd, He'll fill you every day. Don't wait on others to pour back into you; go to the real source. Tammy is my best friend, but God is my source. We don't serve anyone out of our ability but out of His abundance. And sin is like building a dam against the flow. If sin in your life is hindering His flow, get it right today.

The Lord is good. He is able. He offers you a place at the table. Even before you turn the next page of this book, meet Him there. He'll give you more than enough of what you need.

Tammy's Take: Through the years and seasons of life, at times I've felt alone and overwhelmed, with no strength and no energy, too tired to keep pushing forward. During those times, my help came from Christ alone. No human being can heal the deepest anguish of our souls.

God would awaken me during the wee hours of the morning to call me to the darkness, stillness, and quiet of the moment to just sit with Him. I would cry out to Him, pour my heart out to Him, and share with Him my fears, frustrations, failures, hurts, and disappointments.

He didn't scold and chide me; He held me in His strong arms as a father does his child, reassuring me that He saw, He knew, He was working, and He would continue to work in my life for His glory. Not once did He walk away and leave me on my own. He works in ways man is totally incapable of working. He works on our hearts, drawing us into a deeper faith and a deeper relationship with the Lover of our soul, the Author and Finisher of our faith (even through our pain). He's not finished yet. Let's keep our eyes on Him.

Spend some time talking to the Lord about your situation, and then let's continue with our ten practical steps toward caring for our parents. We're halfway there!

6. Decide What Care Is Best

Decisions about the care that's best for a parent are some of the hardest decisions a caregiver faces. Knowing the right doctors to choose, the best in-home help to use, and the best place for your parent to live is hard. We want nothing less than the best for our parents, but with so many options and obstacles, it can be difficult to know what the best is.

> *Decisions about the care that's best for a parent are some of the hardest decisions a caregiver faces.*

Tammy and I remind you again: Pray about each decision you make. That might sound like a simple answer, but it's so important. The Lord knows your options and the factors in deciding between them. He will lead and guide you if you listen to Him. I also want to caution you against the paralysis of analysis. While facing these decisions might be hard and overwhelming, don't analyze so much that you don't make timely decisions. You might have to make some of the hardest decisions of your life, but if you've prayed about them and you're following where the Lord leads, you can trust Him with the outcome.

When choosing doctors and other health care providers, choose people you trust. Talk to others who have been there and hear what they have to say about their experiences. Don't be afraid to get second opinions. It's okay to verify what you're being told.

> *You might have to make some of the hardest decisions of your life, but if you've prayed about them and you're following where the Lord leads, you can trust Him with the outcome.*

More difficult than choosing people to help is choosing the place where your parent will live. "If you aren't facing a crisis already, don't wait until one arises to consider housing, because then you will be left with few choices and little time."[2] Keep your parent in the know on what's going on and what options you're looking into.

When considering whether parents can stay in their home, you have to look at factors like safety, costs, and loneliness. "Home certainly is where the heart is, and it is generally the best place for your parent to be, but at some point it may not be feasible or desirable for your parent to stay in his own home."[3]

If you're having trouble making this decision, consider what Grace Lebow and Barbara Kane wrote in their book *Coping with Your Difficult Older Parent*: "You might be too close to your parent's situation to be objective. If so, hire a neutral third party—a care manager—to weigh the risks and advise you."[4] Sometimes an outside perspective helps us see things we might be missing.

> *It's okay to verify what you're being told.*

"One of the most valuable things parents do for their children is provide a good home—a place where they are nurtured and feel safe. Helping to provide such an environment for older parents, wherever they live, is one of the best things adult children can do to help their parents maintain as much of their independence as long as possible."[5]

I caution you again to be careful about making promises you can't keep throughout this process. When I was eight years old, standing outside the home place, my grandfather looked at me and said, "This was your dad's mom's house when she was young, and then it was your mother's family's house later on. If I leave this place to you and your mother, will you keep it in the family?" I was a little boy! I said yes. I tried to keep that promise, but in the end I could not keep it, so my cousin did.

Another request a parent might make is "Don't ever put me in a nursing home." My dad was in the navy, and he served during the Korean War. Even though he fought in a war, he said the hardest day of his life was when he had to put his mother in a nursing home. She had colon cancer, and because we could no longer give her the medical attention she needed at home, we had no other choice. Sometimes you can have the best of intentions to keep a promise, but you might not be able to.

Whether you're considering a nursing home, an assisted living facility, moving your parent closer to you, or moving your parent into your home, "moving day can be wrenching for everyone. You may feel anxious, sad, guilt-ridden, and uncertain. Your parent may be nervous, depressed, angry, or frightened. Put your own worries aside for the moment so you can empathize with her and reassure her."[6]

As hard as this move is for you, consider how much harder it is for your parent. Your dad might not want to make this move. Your mom might feel like she's losing her independence. Your parents might be leaving the place that's been home for a very long time. "For older parents facing declining health and diminished abilities, the loss of familiar surroundings can be particularly troubling. And for many older parents, the greatest loss occurs when they must leave their home."[7]

Do your research before deciding where your mom or dad will live. Knowing that it will be hard no matter what, be open with your parent about why certain decisions must be made. If it's a temporary move—into your home, for example—let them know it's temporary up front. Consider cost, future health and health care needs (especially if your parent has been diagnosed with a certain disease), sibling support, location, and medical support provided when making this decision. "To have the best chance at remaining in one facility, you can consider...a continuing care retirement community (CCRC), which offers a range of options on one campus, from independent-living apartments to assisted living to a full-scale nursing home."[8] The downside is that continuing care options can be expensive. But many different and good options are out there. Do your research and contact your local agency on aging to see what's available in your area.

I want to conclude this section by saying that if you've moved your parent into a nursing home, I know it was hard to move them there, it's hard to visit them there, and it's hard to think about their being there.

May I share a funny story with you and then give you some encouragement?

I went to a health care facility to visit a church member. She called me "Preach." When I arrived, it was time for her opportunity to go outside and smoke. We went to the door, and they lit her a cigarette, but then they noticed she didn't have on any shoes. They wouldn't let her go outside without her shoes. She looked at me and said, "Preach, hold this." Before I knew it, I was standing there with a cigarette! I prayed, *Lord, please don't let anyone see me.*

I ended up placing the cigarette on a counter, and by the time she got back, it had burned down. She was fit to be tied!

While I hope my story made you laugh, I know just walking through the doors of a nursing home with your parent there might make your heart feel as if it's being torn in two. Hear this from my pastor's heart—it's still important that you go. Even if your parent won't know you're there, you'll know it and God will know it. Even if you don't know if your mother can hear you, talk to her like normal. Ask her about her day and tell her about yours. Pray with

> *Even if your parent won't know you're there, you'll know it and God will know it.*

You can be confident that one day you'll both have a glorious resurrected body and you'll join together around the throne celebrating our great God and King!

her. Whether or not she knows you're there, you'll have to live with it if you didn't go. You'll have no regrets for going.

Be comforted by this fact: If you ever get to a place where you don't know your own name (we never know what's going to happen), if you are saved, your name is written in heaven. God knows your name. And if your loved ones are saved, God knows their names too. He hasn't forgotten them, and we do not grieve as those who have no hope (1 Thessalonians 4:13). You can be confident that one day you'll both have a glorious resurrected body and you'll join together around the throne celebrating our great God and King!

7. Understand That Every Situation Is Different

Several years ago, a great, godly man in our church who was also a faithful leader had gout and arthritis, and he couldn't walk without crutches or a cane. You should have seen the rough shape he was in. Well, then his wife died, and he threw away those crutches! The next thing I knew, he was spry and courting! Not long after that, he called me one night and said, "Preacher, will you meet us at the church? We're getting married!"

I thought the world of both him and his fiancée as well as their families. I asked if they had talked to their children. They had, so I married them. God gave this couple several good years together, and their children did their best to accept the marriage and get along. It was a sweet story.

Your mom or dad might not be dating or considering marriage, but they might be. And that illustrates how every situation is different.

A big issue Tammy and I had with our parents was overmedication. My mom had severe back pain, and the doctor gave her medication she was on for two years, taking it every four hours. (This was the same lady who had never taken more than half the recommended dosage of any medication. She even took half an aspirin.) For those couple of years, she wasn't herself, but the doctors just kept giving her the medicine. Only after surgeries, rehab, and working with the nurses there did she get off it.

Today, we work with a pain management specialist, a physician with special training in evaluation, diagnosis, and treatment of all types of pain. Mom is back to herself and doing better than she has in years.

Overmedication was also a problem with Tammy's dad. He had multiple medical issues, and several different doctors were treating him. Each doctor prescribed something different on top of what he was already taking even though all his medications were listed on his charts. When all his medications—an unbelievable number of them—were taken together, he wasn't acting or feeling like himself.

In the hospital, the doctors said he had dementia. They told our family we needed to put him in an Alzheimer's special-care unit (SCUs), sometimes called a memory care unit, and that he would never get better. Thankfully, after another doctor talked to Tammy's dad for a while, she said, "He doesn't have dementia. I've looked at his medications, and they're interacting with one another." She started taking him off the medications, and within a few days he was back to himself.

Medication can change a person's personality and thinking, and overmedication is a significant issue. If you're concerned about changes in your parent, overmedication could be the problem.

This story, too, illustrates that every situation is different. What you face with your parent will be different from what others face with theirs. For instance, your parent might not be dating or overmedicated, but she might have a gambling issue or he might struggle with depression. "The road to being a caregiver is never the same for two people, even within the same family."[9] So many factors are involved: finances, living situations, personalities, the history of the relationship, and particular diagnoses. There is no way that one answer works for everyone, and that's okay.

Comparison kills contentment. That's a powerful statement. Not only does comparison kill contentment, but in the case of caring for your parent, it can cause unnecessary shame, pressure, or feelings of inadequacy. If your friend was able to work full-time, care for her kids, and allow her mom to move into her home all at the same time, you might feel you should do the same. You might even feel shame or inadequate if you can't.

But the truth might be that your friend was battling depression no one knew about, or that her kids greatly missed spending time with her. The truth might be that your mom needs much more medical attention or your job requires extra hours. As hard as it might be, don't compare yourself to others. Every situation is different. Don't be who you think others want you to be. Be who God calls you to be. Don't decide on care for your parent based on what someone else did. Decide on care based on what God leads you to do.

> *Don't be who you think others want you to be. Be who God calls you to be.*

In John 21, we read a story where Peter says to the Lord, "What about him?" (verse 21 NIV). Jesus had told Peter, "When you were younger you dressed yourself and went where you wanted; but when you are old you will stretch out your hands, and someone else will dress you and lead you where you do not want to go" (verse 18). In verse 19 we read that "Jesus said this to indicate the kind of death by which Peter would glorify God." I'm sure that was a lot for Peter to take in, and like many of us who face hard news, he compared himself to John.

Have you ever thought, *Lord, why can't I have the money Joe has?* Or, *Lord, why won't You heal my mom like You did Jeff's?* This is natural. But verse 22 says Jesus answered, "If I want him to remain alive until I return, what is that to you?"

Hear Jesus's words again: "What is that to you?"

Every caregiving situation is different. The authors of *Coping with*

Your Difficult Older Parent wrote that "well over half the adult children...who came to us for psychotherapy were in a state of stress over their 'difficult' parents. They used the word 'difficult,' not so much because of the physical burden of caring for parents in a state of decline, but because of the emotional drain of trying to help parents who were hard to help."[10] Every one of us can be difficult at some time or another, and just as all our parents have dealt with difficult times with us, we, too, will deal with difficult times with them.

> *You will never regret going where God leads you.*

God is a Good Shepherd. If you're a Christian, He's *your* Good Shepherd. He might be asking you to walk a path your friends aren't walking. He might be leading you through a valley that seems darker than everyone else's. But what's that to you? He's with you, and He's promised to be with you every step of the way. You will never regret going where God leads *you*. He will never lead you where His grace cannot sustain and keep *you*.

Tammy's Take: God knows the exact path He has planned for you. It might not be the path you would have chosen for yourself, yet let me assure you that He'll give you everything you need and will need for this journey.

In December 2005, I was diagnosed with a brain tumor. The neurologist and neurosurgeon said it was inoperable, but a neurosurgeon in Little Rock, Arkansas, agreed to do the surgery because he had developed surgical instruments to get to this part of the brain. God was going ahead of me and providing everything I needed (a courageous, pioneering doctor with knowledge and skill to develop these instruments and do the surgery—check).

After looking at my scans, he said my right carotid artery, which supplies the left side of the brain with blood, appeared to be 100 percent blocked. That seemed impossible, because without it open, I should have had a stroke and died.

When performing a cerebral arteriogram, which is putting contrast into the vessels of the brain to determine blood flow through the brain, he discovered that I have an extra vessel in my brain that connects the right and left hemispheres. He told us I was born with this extra vessel, and it had just been "waiting on this moment." When the right carotid artery closed because of pressure from my brain tumor, a valve opened in this extra vessel and immediately began sending blood to the left side of my brain.

What would I need as an adult? A vessel to send blood to the left side of my brain. What had God already prepared while He was knitting me together in my mother's womb? An extra vessel that would work at the precise moment it was needed—check.

I tell that story to remind you that our God knows exactly what we need today, what we will need next week, next month, next year, and until He calls us home. He also knows what our parent needs, and He has the supply already waiting for us. No amount of worrying or fretting could have supplied my need of an extra vessel or even a doctor to discover it so I could see what my God had been doing even before I was born. No amount of money could have purchased either one. Only a loving Father could supply all my needs according to His riches in glory. If He's sending us on a journey, He's already given us everything we'll need.

I would not have chosen a brain tumor path for myself, nor would I choose one for anyone else, but on that path God led me to discover incredible things about my precious heavenly Father and His care and His provision for me. I would never trade that for anything.

God can be trusted whatever your journey. He's waiting with the supply you need. Trust Him!

8. Say No When You Need To

Do you have a tough time saying no? I do. I love people, I love being around people, and I love being there for people. It takes discipline for me to say no.

No one can do it all. I think some would die trying, but no one can do everything and be everything to everyone. When you try it, you end up not being anything to anyone because you're spread so thin. Saying no is not a sign of weakness. It's not saying that you'll never be willing to do what's been asked. It's just saying it's not possible or perhaps wise at this time.

> *Saying no is not a sign of weakness.*

When caring for a parent, life's other demands don't stop. It would be great if they did, but they don't. Instead, becoming a caregiver adds an extra-large helping on an already full plate. You have to decide what's high priority for you and then make decisions accordingly.

Prioritizing can be hard, but it's so necessary, especially when you're being pulled in many directions. As I said before, if you don't control your calendar, everyone else will. If you don't block time to care for your priorities, chances are you'll never have time to care for them.

What's most important to you? When you're 80, looking back on your life, what do you want to say you did well? Once you answer that question, take a look at your calendar. Does what you spend your time doing reflect your answer?

Scripture has a good bit to say about prioritizing. In Matthew 5–6, Jesus is teaching His disciples about all sorts of practical things. He talks to them about being salt and light; about anger, adultery, and divorce; about loving their enemies and giving to the needy; and about how to pray and fast. All of this is part of the famous Sermon on the Mount. If ever there was a sermon that applied to life, this is it!

After teaching on these things, He said,

> Do not store up for yourselves treasures on earth, where moth and rust destroy and where thieves break in and steal. But store up for yourselves treasures in heaven, where neither moth nor rust destroys, and where thieves don't break in and steal. For where your treasure is, there your

heart will be also...You cannot serve both God and money. (Matthew 6:19-21,24 csb)

Maybe you've heard these verses before. Jesus was reminding the people where their priorities should be. Earthly things will pass away, but what's done for eternity will last. What of only earthly value is taking your time? What are you doing that's of eternal value?

In the next verses, Jesus said,

> Therefore I tell you, do not worry about your life, what you will eat or drink; or about your body, what you will wear. Is not life more than food, and the body more than clothes? Look at the birds of the air; they do not sow or reap or store away in barns, and yet your heavenly Father feeds them. Are you not much more valuable than they? Can any one of you by worrying add a single hour to your life? And why do you worry about clothes? See how the flowers of the field grow. They do not labor or spin. Yet I tell you that not even Solomon in all his splendor was dressed like one of these. If that is how God clothes the grass of the field, which is here today and tomorrow is thrown into the fire, will he not much more clothe you—you of little faith? (Matthew 6:25-30 niv).

As He concludes this topic, He says, "But seek first his kingdom and his righteousness, and all these things will be given to you as well" (verse 33 niv). *Seek first.* Jesus tells us what our *first* priority should be. When we seek Him, everything else falls into place.

Are you worried or stressed about figuring everything out with your parent? Are you concerned about *how* things are going to get done and *when* they're going to happen and *who* is going to do it? Seek Him first. We're set free from worry when we lay our needs before Him.

Do you need to say no to anything so you can put Jesus first in your life? Do you need to say no to something that's taking up your time but has no eternal value? Make God a priority.

You've heard the saying "Only do what only you can do." Sometimes daily tasks that take up so much of your time can be done by someone else. Sure, some tasks are urgent; they need to be done. But they're not necessarily important for *you* to do.

When you consider how to spend the hours in your day, contemplate these helpful tips:

Only *you* can be a mom or dad to your kids. That might mean you pay someone else to clean your house so your free time is spent with them.

Only *you* can be a husband to your wife or a wife to your husband. That might mean letting someone else host the Bible study so you and your spouse can simply attend.

Only *you* can be a child to your parent. That might mean letting someone else do physical therapy with them so your time with them isn't spent arguing over exercising.

Think through who and what are priority for you. What tasks can others help with so you can focus on your priorities? It's okay to say no to some things you've always done. It's okay to say no to things people prefer you to do. Saying no to things others can do allows you to keep the main things the main things. It allows you to say yes to something more important.

> *Sometimes you might have to say no to your parent.*

Sometimes you might have to say no to your parent. This can be so hard! Maybe their car keys need to be taken away or it's no longer safe for them to cook. Just like you had to say no to protect your children when they were young, you might have to say no to your parent for her own safety or your own safety (physical) or sanity (emotional). If you're met with resistance, recruit help from those around you. Enlist your support team to do just that—support you.

While our parents are not our children, this season of caring for them can have similarities to caring for our own children. Sometimes I told my children they couldn't do something they really wanted to do, but I did that for their safety and protection. It was difficult for them to understand, but it was also difficult for Tammy and me to stop them. It was like the line we all heard from our parents: "This hurts me more than it hurts you."

> *Don't let guilt or fear of letting people down force you to overcommit or make decisions you know aren't best.*

Remember to honor and respect a parent in how you treat them. Don't be condescending or hateful when you have to step in. Saying no is prioritizing their safety and protection and possibly the safety of those around them.

Throughout your time caregiving, no doubt you'll have to say no. You might hate it; others might not like it; but it will be necessary. Don't let guilt or fear of letting people down force you to overcommit or make decisions you know aren't best. Before you wear yourself too thin or allow yourself to be swayed by others, determine your priorities. Remind yourself that saying no isn't a sign of weakness but an act of love.

9. Use Technology

One of the young pastors on our staff was telling me about how he was dating a girl who didn't live close by. He said they use FaceTime to communicate, and he mentioned how nice it was that they could see each other while they were talking. Then he paused, and after a moment proceeded to define what he meant by FaceTime in what I'll call kindergarten terms.

Well, while I'm not an IT expert, I do know about FaceTime. I have a smartphone, an iPad, and a Mac computer, and I consider myself somewhat (key word: *somewhat*) tech savvy. But whether or not you're tech savvy, technology can be a huge help to you while caring for your parent.

Technology offers us resources just like senior centers or local agencies on aging do—a whole pool of them. "Mobile technology is transforming the way people work, play, and receive medical care. In 2011, more than two-thirds of caregivers were using some form of technology to help them with caregiving, including Web-based calendars, social media, smartphone apps that manage calendar appointments, medication refills, telemedicine visits, and medical hotlines."[11]

Think of the advantages today.

Years ago Apple used a catchy phrase in advertisements for the iPhone: "There's an app for that." Most of us might not have known it at the time, but that's so true. Years later, especially with more and more people owning smartphones or tablets, there really are apps, or at least online resources, for just about everything.

Depending on how technologically inclined your mother is, she could be using online tools already. If she is, you're already one step ahead. The key is having access to her accounts.

Does your father pay any bills online? Does he use email or social media? Does he have a smartphone? If so, these are all accounts you'll need access to. Recreating accounts or trying to get access to an account when it's too late can be difficult. While your parent is still able to share, ask her to work with you on making a list of accounts and passwords.

Following is a sample list taken from *The Caregiver's Toolbox* to help you think through what usernames and passwords you'll need. Keep this information in a safe place.

- health care accounts
- health savings accounts
- insurance accounts
- computers
- mobile devices
- internet services
- airline memberships

- car rental memberships
- hotel memberships
- AARP/AAA memberships
- television passwords
- Web passwords
- internet SSID
- modem passwords to access the Web
- identity protection services
- computer backup
- Kindle library
- frequent shopping sites (eBay, Amazon, etc.)
- iTunes
- Facebook/Twitter/Pinterest/Instagram/other social media[12]

Once you have access to your parent's accounts, you can more easily help with paying bills, transferring account ownership, closing accounts, and so on. Doing this all online will save you a significant amount of time, and in some cases, headache. You don't have to go to each location, determine the right person to talk to, and wait for that person to be available, only to find out you left an important paper you need at home.

If your parent doesn't do much online, you can still create online accounts for him. Does he have to mail a check to pay his cable bill each month? You can set up a recurring payment online so that neither of you has to remember when it's due or worry about the post office misplacing the envelope. Online accounts for banking, insurance, medical records, and the like keep track of history. You don't have to sort through papers to find when a bill or a doctor's fee was paid—you can just look online.

Another benefit of online work is that you have records of the transactions: changes made, payments made, and even questions asked. If you talk to someone on the phone and receive inaccurate information, it's your word against theirs. You can also manage business online from anywhere. You don't have to be at your parent's home or even in town.

If you need assistance with online accounts, consult your kids or grandkids. They can be a huge help with the latest technology. You can also talk to the company directly about using their online services. Online tutorials are often available as well. Most online sources are user friendly once you become familiar with them. It's also usually hard to mess everything up with one click! Don't worry about that. Just read carefully as you go and ask questions when needed.

Various online resources can be helpful outside of what you or your parent might already employ. For example, you'll find tools for nutrition and exercise. Are you trying to keep track of your parent's diet or encourage her to exercise? You can use apps that help you track data right at your fingertips. Are you trying to coordinate a caregiving schedule for your dad? Do you want to coordinate meals for him? Tools are available for that too. Do you need to refill a prescription? You can with the touch of a button.

Has your parent ever video-chatted? This could be a way to connect with family members who don't live nearby. Even email can be enjoyable. Family can send pictures and encouraging notes. One lady in our church was on hospice for more than a year. She was a godly woman who loved her family and church family. During that year, her iPad was a great tool for her. She received photos from family and friends. She had a shortcut to watch sermons online, and she faithfully watched them every week from the hospital bed in her home. She even played games and perused Pinterest when someone taught her how to do that. She couldn't get out, and people couldn't physically visit her every day, but she could stay connected.

Technology can help you with basic home tasks such as turning lights off and on. Security cameras and door locks can be controlled from your phone or computer. Reminders can be set for taking medication. Some medical practices offer virtual visits, when you don't have to physically go to their offices.

The resources are endless! Talk to those around you who use technology and find out what will work for you. *The Caregivers Toolbox* is also a great resource for reading more about how technology can benefit caregivers and parents. Some of the tips we've given, and will give below, are also found in that book, as well as a variety of others. Don't be afraid to try something new; you might find it's a significant help.

Security is important when using technology. These tools can be wonderful, but be smart when using them. Have good antivirus software on your computer. Set strong passwords for all of your accounts. Don't autosave them but type them in each time. Use software and apps from reliable sources. Don't give out personal information, especially if you question why it's needed. For example, your doctor's office or insurance company might need your Social Security number, but it wouldn't make sense for an app that tracks your exercise to need it.

Have a plan in place in case your device is lost or stolen. "Set up features to find your smartphone or shut down specific features in the event it is stolen or lost. Most likely, your smartphone has confidential information that could identify you."[13] If you keep all of your information on your phone, have a backup somewhere.

Just as with any other type of security, use common sense as best you can. If something doesn't feel okay to you, don't do it. If you get a message that seems odd, don't click it. If you're unsure, check with someone who knows.

Technology can be an immense help to you during this season. It can save you time, money, and resources. It can be a fun and practical tool for your parent and for you as well. Don't be afraid to try it and figure out what can work for you and your family.

10. Remember the Best and Forget the Rest

As parents age, they can change. Disease, fatigue, loneliness, and other factors can cause them to act in ways that aren't normal. Your mom or dad might not even know your name or remember who you are.

She might say or do things she would never have said or done before. He might not treat you the way he used to treat you. These acts could be embarrassing to you, or just flat out difficult, but they can also be hurtful.

No matter the struggle you're facing with your parent, I encourage you to remember the best and forget the rest. Focus on the good days and the positive instead of on the bad days and the negative. Virginia Morris suggests,

> *Focus on the good days and the positive instead of on the bad days and the negative.*

> If your parent is quite ill, if he has gotten crotchety in his old age, or if dementia has distorted his personality, find a photo from when he was younger—a photo of him at his best, a photo of him holding you when you were a child, a photo of him strong and well. Or put together a collage of photos. Then put it on your refrigerator or on your desk, someplace where you will see it often. It will help you remember better times, when he was stronger. It will help you recall the father who laughed with you and cared for you and taught you things. It will help you remember why you are doing so much for him now.[14]

Thankfully, the Lord focuses on the positive for us. In Isaiah 43:25 He says, "I, even I, am he who blots out your transgressions, for my own sake, and remembers your sins no more" (NIV). The Lord forgives us. Because Jesus paid the price for our sin on the cross, the Lord chooses to remember our sin no more. This doesn't mean He forgets them, but He no longer holds them against us.

Because of His forgiveness to us, then, we can forgive others. Stop saying, "I can forgive, but I can never forget." Stop replaying the offense over and over. Forgive and let it go. God's constant forgiveness and love in our lives and the power of the Holy Spirit working in us enable us to forgive and love others. He fills us so that we can pour out and give. The Lord never leaves us empty if we look to Him.

Through Him, not only can we love and forgive, but we can choose to dwell on the positive. We can choose to focus on images in our minds of good times with our parents. We can choose to put away thoughts of fear or disease or death or hurt or bitterness. Paul wrote, "The weapons we fight with are not the weapons of the world. On the contrary, they have divine power to demolish strongholds. We demolish arguments and every pretension that sets itself up against the knowledge of God, and we take captive every thought to make it obedient to Christ" (2 Corinthians 10:4-5 NIV).

> *God's constant forgiveness and love in our lives and the power of the Holy Spirit working in us enables us to forgive and love others.*

What are thoughts that are obedient to Christ? Philippians 4:8 says, "Whatever is true, whatever is noble, whatever is right, whatever is pure, whatever is lovely, whatever is admirable—if anything is excellent or praiseworthy—think about such things" (NIV).

Tammy's Take: This verse from Philippians is displayed in my bathroom. Each morning when I am getting ready for the day, there it is staring at me. On some days, it's easy to live out in my life, heart, and mind. On other days, those difficult struggling days, I can choose to either obey God's words to me or reject them.

Have you ever just wanted to indulge in anger, frustration, and self-pity? Sounds crazy, doesn't it? But that's what we choose to do when we refuse to think on the true, noble, right, pure, lovely, admirable, excellent, and praiseworthy things. Some days, it's hard for us to capture thoughts that are running wild. That's when we must fall into the arms of Jesus—asking Him to give us His thoughts, His perspective, His grace and love that He so kindly lavishes upon us.

If you're walking through yuck right now, ask Him to remind you of a sweet time, a joyous time, a funny time, a time when He came through for you. Before you know it, you'll find yourself with a grateful heart, trusting the One who will once again carry you through.

What negative thoughts do you have toward your parent? What are you not forgiving your mother or father for? What do you replay in your mind that's not pleasing to God? What images of your parent are you focusing on that are full of sickness and disease? Ask the Lord to help you put that away. Ask Him to help you put the truth of His love and forgiveness in your mind and to replace the negative with the positive. Through Him, and only through Him, we *can* remember the best and forget the rest.

6

Heaven

Surely goodness and mercy shall follow me all the days of my life;
and I will dwell in the house of the LORD forever.
PSALM 23:6

I pray that the preceding chapters have left you feeling more encouraged, helped, and equipped to care for your parent. I pray this chapter, as we talk about your parent's final days, will be the most powerful yet.

Every person on this earth will face death. You will. I will. Your parent will. Even though we know death is inevitable, it's still hard! "For many caregivers and their families, the days and weeks preceding a parent's death can be the most difficult part of the journey. Not only does it represent the end of the caregiving relationship, it means the end of the parent-child relationship as well."[1]

Praise God for the hope He gives. Remember Psalm 23:4? "Yea, though I walk through the valley of the shadow of death, I will fear no evil; for you are with me; Your rod and Your staff, they comfort me." If the Lord is your Shepherd and your parent is nearing death, you do not have to fear. You can rest assured that He will be right there comforting you.

I received the letter below from a church member who spent more than six years caring for her mother-in-law:

Hello, Pastor Grant!

Dave's mother moved to Virginia from Connecticut in 2010. She was 86 at the time...We were her transportation and appointment makers. We ordered all her prescriptions, we handled all of the medical insurance, and Dave took care of her finances. We have four children, and this was like having the responsibility of a fifth child...We took her out to eat with us and had her over to eat at our house quite often. She also spent every holiday with us...

Dave's mother passed away in February. She lived a long 92 years and was able to be near family and spend most of her time with us those last six-and-a-half years of her life. Dave also had the privilege of talking to her about God, and she was saved while she lived here near us.

There were so many things we were not prepared for prior to taking care of an elderly parent...Not everyone gets the privilege of caring for an elderly parent or a special needs child, but those of us that do learn that we can do none of it without God and His constant presence in our life. It takes a lot of prayer and dependence on God and family support.

In Christ,
Diane

No doubt, those years were hard. But did you catch the line right in the middle? "Dave also had the privilege of talking to her about God, and she was saved while she lived here near us." Wow!

> *While the end of this season of caring for your parent will be difficult, it can also be sweet.*

While the end of this season of caring for your parent will be difficult, it can also be sweet. When the fact that they won't be around forever is immediately before you, what they mean to you becomes increasingly evident.

The seriousness of their death can also

become pressing. If you've never talked to your parent about the Lord, this is the time. You can give them no greater gift than to lead them to know the Lord as their Shepherd. No fear in death is only for those who know Him.

Surely Goodness and Mercy Shall Follow Me All the Days of My Life

Finishing up our look at Psalm 23, the last verse says, "Surely goodness and mercy shall follow me all the days of my life; and I will dwell in the house of the LORD forever." Because of Jesus, we can be satisfied in life, safe in death, and secure for eternity. "Surely" is not a question, but an exclamation. For the Christian, the best *is* yet to come.

> *Because of Jesus, we can be satisfied in life, safe in death, and secure for eternity.*

Goodness and mercy are with you even now. Not everything in life is good, but God is good, and He works all things together for good for those who love Him and have been "called according to His purpose" (Romans 8:28). "All the days of my life" means *all* days. It means the day you were born, the day you will die, each day you care for your parent, sunny days, and rainy days. God will give you goodness and mercy *all* of your days.

I Will Dwell in the House of the Lord Forever

The last part of verse 6 says, "I will dwell in the house of the LORD forever." For the Christian, death is not the end. *Dwell* means "to go home." This world is not our home. When we die, we'll just be getting started in a place with no more death, or mourning, or crying, or pain. In a place where we'll see the Lord Jesus face-to-face and worship Him forever.

In addition to encouraging you to talk to your parent about the

Lord, I encourage you to let them know what they mean to you. Your words don't have to be eloquent, and you don't have to be long-winded. You can even write down what you want to say on paper and give it to them (or read what you've written to them if they're no longer able to read). There is something to say for words on paper.

Even if you've never been one to share much of your emotions before, if your feelings are at the surface, take advantage of that. Don't hold back expressing your love or appreciation for your parents. Honor your father with your words. You won't regret it, and he might share in return, creating a memory you will cherish forever. I've heard many stories of families and relationships restored during sickness, death, or crisis. If you allow it, this difficult season can be more special and treasured than you would ever think.

You can also talk to your parent about funeral arrangements. If your mother hasn't already planned her funeral or memorial service, help her do so. This is another way to honor her, but also to help yourself. "Funerals are highly emotional events that too often take place with very little time for planning. Emotional purchases usually result in higher costs. Consider yourself fortunate if you and your loved one have pre-planned the funeral, as it is one of the greatest acts of love a dying person can offer to his or her caregiver and family."[2] Tammy and I both have already planned our funerals. I encourage you to plan yours and to work with your parent on planning theirs.

Try to be present as much as you can during a parent's last days. Tammy was able to spend quality time with her dad before he passed away. She tried to honor whatever he asked. If he wanted to go for a ride, she took him. If he wanted homemade ice cream, she made it, and then they'd sit on the back porch as they ate it. Whatever he wanted, she tried to do.

We were also both present when our dads died. That's not the case for everyone. So many people were present for days or weeks but then had to leave before their parent died. They can feel cheated or robbed, but death is in God's hands; He decides when to call us home. A parent might even choose not to die in front of their child. There's no reason to feel guilty if that is the case for you. If you've made every effort to be there for your mom or dad, that's all you can do.

If parents who know Jesus and are saved are very sick, impending death can be a blessing to them. You can keep them comfortable and ask God to be merciful to them. Tell them it's okay to go. Release them, and let Jesus be your peace.

Jesus said,

> Let not your heart be troubled; you believe in God, believe also in Me. In My Father's house are many mansions; if it were not so, I would have told you. I go to prepare a place for you. And if I go and prepare a place for you, I will come again and receive you to Myself; that where I am, there you may be also...I am the way, the truth, and the life. No one comes to the Father except through Me." (John 14:1-3,6)

Both my dad and Tammy's dad had a glimpse of heaven before they died. My dad's glimpse was brief. Tammy's dad's glimpse involved a lot more detail.

At the hospital one night, we all thought her dad was dying. The nurses dimmed the lights, and they put a sign on the door so no one would interrupt us. But as he was lying in the bed, her dad suddenly said, "Oooh-wee!"

Up until that point, he'd been so weak that he hadn't been saying much. When Tammy asked him what it was, he sat up a little bit, stretched out his hands, and said, "I am on the steps of glory. This is the most magnificent moment of my life."

We think he's dying, and he says it's the most magnificent moment of his life! What assurance that there is no fear in death for those who are in Christ.

A minute or two later, he put his hands on his head and said, "Oooh-wee. You just won't believe it. Glory, glory, hallelujah. Glory,

glory, hallelujah." He said that a few times and then said as he looked and pointed up, "Thank you that I have a Savior who stands between me and Him to take me where He is."

We were all shocked and listening intently as he kept describing what he was seeing. "There are so many people here. Look at all the babies. Look at all the lights. It's so beautiful!" He kept referring to the Savior and saying, "Glory, glory, hallelujah."

The only time he started to cry was when he said, "Jesus, please forgive me for not telling everybody I've ever come in contact with about this beautiful place, because You love them just as much as You love me." Then in a few minutes, he finally said, "Now, we are going to ask our pastor to dismiss us in prayer."

Tammy asked him about what he had just said, and he snapped his fingers in my direction and said a little more firmly, "We are going to ask our *pastor* to dismiss us in prayer." I had my laptop out and was still typing away, my head down. Finally, he said, "Grant, get over here and pray!"

I got up and went to his bed. We prayed, and then he said, "That was the most amazing worship service I have ever been in, in my life!"

He didn't pass away that night; he got a little better after that. He wanted to get up, which he hadn't done in days. He wanted to eat, which he also hadn't done. He wanted to call people and tell them about what he'd seen. He'd been in the presence of the Lord, and it gave him a new strength and energy that none of us could explain. He ended up going home, and he lived a few more weeks. It was such a sweet time of being ushered into the presence of the Lord. We had such a celebration at his funeral!

Often when a person has been sick, someone will say at their funeral, "At least they're not suffering anymore." That's only true if they know Jesus. It's only true if they're in heaven. With both of our dads, that was the case.

Think about this for a minute. If you die lost, apart from Jesus, this world is as close to heaven as you'll ever get. If you're saved, however, this world is as close to hell as you will ever get. I don't want you to finish this book without making sure that *you* know Jesus and that *you* know *you* will spend eternity in heaven with Him, and that heaven will be *your* home one day. Right where you are, search your heart. Do you have assurance that when you die heaven will be your home? If not, you can pray right where you are. Here's a sample prayer for you:

> *Dear Lord Jesus, I believe You are the way, the truth, and the life. You've said no one comes to the Father except through You. I'm trusting in You and You alone to take me to heaven. I'm not trusting in religion or good works, but I trust in the cross and Your sacrificial, substitutionary death on my behalf for forgiveness of my sins. I believe You rose from the dead, and I ask You to be my Lord and Savior. I repent of my sins, and I turn my life over to You. However long I have left here on this earth, help me live a life that's pleasing to You. Thank You for hearing my prayer and saving my soul. In Jesus's name, amen.*

Trusting Jesus is the best decision you will ever make. He's the one who will get you through the days ahead. He's the one who will lead you through this valley of death to green pastures and still waters. If you just prayed that prayer, I join with the angels in heaven and rejoice with you (Luke 15:10).

Though I don't know you, I've prayed for you. I've prayed that your time of caring for your parent will be sweet, and that it will be a time when your entire family grows closer to one another and closer to the Lord. I pray that these days, though hard, will be good, cherished days, and that God's grace will abound for you and your parent. You are loved. And you will survive the road ahead.

Tammy's Take: Death is not the end. As believers, we'll be reunited with our loved ones one day—in a land with no more sorrow and no more tears for the former things are wiped away and all things have become new. A new chapter begins with no more sickness and no more suffering. But for now, until then, cling tightly to the Savior. He will carry you through. Thank Him that He's allowing you this time with your parent. Some people lose their loved one suddenly, not gifted with walking with them through the last pages of life. Lovingly walk with your mother or father to the very gates of glory. You'll never regret it!

30 Days *of* Encouragement

Introduction

The following 30 devotionals are for your encouragement as you care for your parent, and we'll tell you more about them shortly. But seeking God is what we believe is most important as you walk this path. Here's how:

Spend Time in the Word

Find a place away from distractions and read Scripture or use an audio Bible. You can't know the ways of God apart from the Word of God, and you can't cling to the words of encouragement there unless you hear them.

Matthew 4:4 says, "It is written: 'Man shall not live on bread alone, but on every *word* that comes from the mouth of God.'" Nor can you live on stress-induced adrenaline. You need the Word of God.

Spend Time in Prayer

If the apostle Paul needed to pray, and Jesus the Son of God needed to pray, how much more do we need to pray? You might say, "I don't know what to pray." Then pray the Word. Read passages from the Bible *to* the Lord, claiming His promises as you do.

Or you might say, "With so many demands on me now, I don't have much time to pray." The important thing is that you pray, not how long you pray. Pray continuously throughout the day as you drive, or as you dress, or as you care for your parent.

In each of these devotions, we've given you a verse or verses for the day, some applications, and often suggestions for what to pray about or do. Because of all you're going through, we've made it easy for you to spend time in the Word and time in prayer.

You might also want to use a devotional, a one-year Bible, a free app on your phone, or a variety of other tools. But even if you do, we encourage you to use these 30 devotions as well. They're specifically written for those of you caring for parents, and we believe you'll find them helpful. If you choose not to read them, please still commit to spending time in the Word and in prayer every day for the next month. Again, we encourage you to seek God—and His encouragement—in your caregiving journey.

A Few Tips Before You Begin

Here are a few tips we've put together for you. These are often things I share with people in our church who ask about getting the most out of their devotional time.

1. *Pray before you read.* Ask God to speak and to reveal Himself to you. Ask Him to help you stay focused, to help you understand what you read, and to help you apply it to your life.

2. *Take your time.* Don't try to just squeeze in the day's devotion. Allow yourself enough time. If possible, look up the passage cited and respond to what the Lord might be saying to you.

3. *Read the Scripture.* Scripture is the most important part of each piece. Read it before the devotion so you'll have the context intended.

4. *Take in the applications.* Consider each item and ask the Lord how He would have you apply what you read.

5. *Obey what the Lord leads you to do.* It's great to be encouraged

as you read, but putting what you read into practice is even better. Commit to follow through on God's leading.

We pray that the next 30 days will mark a significant period of encouragement in both your spiritual and caregiving journeys. As the people were told in Deuteronomy 31:8, "The LORD...goes before you. He will be with you, He will not leave you nor forsake you."

Here's one more thing I'd like for you to remember: Caring for a parent isn't about only your parent. It's about you too.

Day 1

Ask God to Work

LORD, I have heard of your fame; I stand in awe of your deeds, LORD.
Repeat them in our day, in our time make them known.
Habakkuk 3:2 NIV

While caring for a parent, you'll no doubt experience twists and turns, battles, and testing. But let me begin our 30 days with this encouragement: God will never leave you nor forsake you. He will raise up people to help you along the way. He will fight battles for you, and He will make a way when there seems to be no way.

In other words, He'll do for you what He did for the people of Israel.

The story of God leading the Israelites to the land He promised is also full of twists and turns, battles, and testing. But God moved in powerful ways. He fulfilled promises to individuals, raised up mighty leaders, fought battles for His people, set captives free, parted waters.

In chapter 3 of the book of Habakkuk, the prophet reminisces about God's great works. But he also asks the Lord to "repeat them in our day." If Habakkuk could ask God to work, why can't we?

We can—and God expects such prayers!

Jonathan Edwards, a great theologian and key figure in the Great Awakening, said, "So [it] is God's will, through his wonderful grace, that the prayers of his saints should be one great and principal means of carrying on the designs of Christ's kingdom in the world. When God has something very great to accomplish for his church [and I would add, for us as individuals], it is his will that there should precede it the extraordinary prayers of his people."[1]

Remember God's works from the past. Then ask Him to work now, in the present. Don't be afraid to ask for what you need as a caregiver. And if you're not quite sure what you need, use these next 30 days for discovery.

Application

* Ask God to move mightily as you care for your parent.

* Commit to praying every day, praising God and unafraid to ask for what you need.

Day 2

Sing

I waited patiently for the LORD; and He inclined to me, and heard my cry.
He also brought me up out of a horrible pit, out of the miry clay,
and set my feet upon a rock, and established my steps.
He has put a new song in my mouth.
Psalm 40:1-3

What an encouraging testimony of praise in the passage above! While we don't know everything David had been through or was facing when he wrote this psalm, we can gather a few turbulent details from Psalm 40. The situations he was in

- required waiting (verse 1)
- seemed horrible (verse 2)
- surrounded him with trouble (verse 12)
- involved sin (verse 12)
- included heartbreak (verse 12)
- invoked enemies (verses 14-15)

What a mess! Notice, however, what David says the Lord did for him. First, He lifted David out of the trouble he was in, and then He established his steps. More, He put a new song of praise in his mouth.

No matter what troubling circumstances you're in, no matter whether you've had a relationship with God for a long time or you're just beginning (James 4:8 says, "Draw near to God and He will draw near to you"), God can lift you out, show you the way, and give you a new song.

Tammy often sang to or with our dads in their last days. Music can change the atmosphere. If your caregiving journey has been at all turbulent or even just challenging, ask the Lord for a new song—in your heart (Ephesians 5:19 refers to "making melody in your heart to the Lord") but also perhaps on your lips.

Application

* Ask the Lord to give you a new song as He guides you through this journey.

* Try singing to or with your parent or playing praise music.

Day 3

Trust Who Holds the Future

Moses summoned Joshua and said to him in the presence
of all Israel, "Be strong and courageous, for you must go
with this people into the land that the LORD swore to their
ancestors to give them... The LORD himself goes before
you and will be with you; he will never leave you nor
forsake you. Do not be afraid; do not be discouraged."
Deuteronomy 31:7-8 NIV

Fear of the future can paralyze us, perhaps especially when we're responsible for the well-being of a parent. If this is the first time (many of us care for one parent and then for the other), we're dealing with a responsibility we've never faced before. We can fret and worry so much about what might happen—surgeries, relocation, loss—that we freeze and don't accomplish much of anything.

In the verses above, Moses is handing over his responsibilities to Joshua, whose responsibility it would be to lead the people of Israel into the promised land—no easy task. Put yourself in his shoes. The Israelites were a mess. They had a history of complaining and grumbling, of growing impatient and worshipping other gods. On top of that, the area was occupied, and Joshua would be leading military efforts to obtain the land.

Joshua had to be overwhelmed. He probably had a thousand what-if questions, maybe similar to some of yours today. But speaking from firsthand experience, Moses assures Joshua, "The LORD himself goes before you and will be with you" (verse 8). Moses had seen this truth time and time again. He knew the Lord could be trusted with the future.

No matter what task God has given you, including parenting your parent, you can be sure He sees and goes before you. Nothing catches Him off guard. He has already made provision, and He can be trusted with not only your parent's future but with yours.

Application

* Praise God that He knows the plans He has for you and your parent, and that He has already provided the means to accomplish those plans.

* Commit to trusting God with any fear about the future that may be paralyzing you.

Day 4

Put the Past in Its Place

Do not dwell on the past. See, I am doing a new thing!
Now it springs up; do you not perceive it? I am making
a way in the wilderness and streams in the wasteland.
Isaiah 43:18-19 NIV

Fear of the future can paralyze us, and so can dwelling on a mistake, a situation, or a hurt from our past. What's paralyzing you might involve your parent. Perhaps an apology from your mom or an apology accepted by your dad is what you hope for. Unfortunately, that doesn't always happen.

Yet the Bible says God's mercies (*compassions* in the NIV) are new each morning (Lamentations 3:23). And in Isaiah 43:18-19, He told the people not to dwell on the past. After all, He was doing a new thing and making a way.

When the Israelites were crossing the Red Sea, the Lord moved from leading them in front to following behind them. What an awesome picture. He protected them from where they had been, ensuring their freedom from past slavery. He placed His presence behind them, declaring once and for all that Pharaoh and the Egyptians could no longer touch them.

He does the same for us. When we are in Christ, He comes behind and declares that once and for all, the past can no longer have a hold on us. We just have to let it go.

What is in your past is *past*. What's in your parent's past is past. It's all done, and God wants to do a new thing for you and your parent. He wants to make a way, helping you put the past in its place and grasp the new present He provides.

Application

* Identify anything you've been dwelling on from your past, especially if it involves your parent. Ask for and accept God's forgiveness and healing.

* Praise God for the new thing He wants to do in and through you even if you're not yet sure what that new thing is.

Day 5

His Best Is Best

To Him who is able to do exceedingly abundantly
above all that we ask or think...
Ephesians 3:20

Sometimes in the midst of caregiving, we can become discouraged (or paralyzed) when we don't see how or when a challenging situation will work out, when we can't figure out every detail of a plan, when we don't have all the answers we'd like to have.

Worse, we can be tempted to cut back, to stop giving our parent who needs care our best because our best never seems to be enough. We can even be tempted to quit, to hope someone else will take on this responsibility. And yet, what would have happened if the Israelites had quit? What if they had given up hope when they came to the Red Sea? They certainly would not have seen God move in such a mighty way on their behalf.

If you ever feel so discouraged that you think you might as well stop trying or even quit, hear these words from the Lord: "As the heavens are higher than the earth, so are my ways higher than your ways and my thoughts than your thoughts" (Isaiah 55:9 NIV).

I doubt the Israelites could have imagined that the Lord would part the Red Sea for them. Seriously, who would have? But He did. He went beyond what they could have ever thought. And He'll do that for you. You don't have to know how everything will work out. You don't have to know every detail of every plan. You don't need all the answers. You just have to keep going with what you *do* know.

The Lord can "do exceedingly abundantly above all that we ask or think" (Ephesians 3:20). Trust Him. Keep going. Persevere. He's at work, and His best is the best.

Application

* Thank the Lord that His thoughts are higher than yours as you walk through this season. Praise Him because His best is best.

* Ask God to do exceedingly and abundantly more than you could ask or think as you care for your parent.

Day 6

Why Faith?

*Faith is confidence in what we hope for
and assurance about what we do not see.*
Hebrews 11:1 NIV

We've talked about fear of the future, pulls from the past, and questions without answers, all of which can come up when we're faced with the challenge of caring for a parent. Those obstacles are all real, and they evoke real emotions.

The Israelites, whose journey we've been using to illustrate what we can learn for our caregiving journeys, were real people. They had all the same fears and emotions people have today. And Hebrews 11:29 gives us a clear picture of what got them through: "By faith the people passed through the Red Sea."

What exactly is faith? Hebrews 11:1 tells us "faith is confidence in what we hope for and assurance about what we do not see" (NIV). The Israelites chose to be confident in the hope God had given them. They made up their minds to believe His promises, and that's what we must do in challenging times—believe. Belief leads to faith.

To persevere through a demanding time, to stay the course, we must have faith. We must believe God, taking Him at His word and trusting that He will go before us and come behind us. We must believe that He can do beyond what we could ever ask or think.

As you care for your parent, you might find your faith challenged, shaky, even slipping away. Don't let that happen. Be like the Israelites at the Red Sea. Choose to be confident in the hope God offers. Make up your mind to believe His promises.

May your prayer be that of the apostles: "Increase our faith!" (Luke 17:5).

Tomorrow we'll look at how to *live* by faith.

Application

　＊ If you wonder how faith makes a difference, remember how God parted the Red Sea for the Israelites.

　＊ Ask the Lord to help you increase your faith—even a little. Jesus said, "If you have faith as a mustard seed, you will say to this mountain, 'Move from here to there,' and it will move; and nothing will be impossible for you" (Matthew 17:20).

Day 7

Lived-Out Faith

By faith the people passed through the Red Sea as on dry land.
Hebrews 11:29 NIV

The book of Hebrews not only tells us what faith is but gives us examples of how people lived out their faith—and not just the Israelites at the Red Sea. Read the eleventh chapter of Hebrews. "By faith" is a phrase used over and over as the author tells us about people in the Old Testament who did or experienced amazing things. Their situations weren't any easier than the Israelites.

God called Abraham to go where "he did not know where he was going" (verse 8). Sarah was past childbearing age but desperately wanted a child (verse 11). Moses's parents were afraid for their son's life (verse 23). Moses was at risk of being mistreated (verse 25). These were challenging situations, yet all these people had faith in God, and the Lord honored their faith and moved powerfully.

The author of Hebrews had so many examples of people with a lived-out faith that he ran out of time to name them all. But he referred to those "who through faith conquered kingdoms, administered justice, and gained what was promised; who shut the mouths of lions, quenched the fury of the flames, and escaped the edge of the sword; whose weakness was turned to strength; and who became powerful in battle and routed foreign armies" (verses 33-34).

Living by faith isn't necessarily easy, and faith is not having faith *in* faith. It's choosing daily to take God at His word *for that day*. It's putting one foot in front of the other and continuously following Him. That's what these heroes of faith did. They chose to believe God over what was logical. They chose to hope in Him more than fearing earthly consequences, even if they never saw the promise fully fulfilled. The Bible says the Lord commended them for it.

Oh, that we would have faith that the Lord commends and uses to make an eternal difference. Faith is so important that we'll take it up again on Day 22.

Application

* Ask the Lord to help you develop a lived-out faith.

* Ask God to use you even as you care for your parent, just as He used the people in Hebrews 11.

Day 8

Finding Soul Rest

My soul, find rest in God.
Psalm 62:5 NIV

Maybe you're doing everything you can to care for yourself so you're in shape to care for your parent, but that doesn't mean you don't need the "soul rest" that comes only from God.

David knew this rest: "The LORD...makes me to lie down in green pastures; He leads me beside the still waters" (Psalm 23:1-2). For both those in need of physical rest and those in need of soul rest, Isaiah proclaimed, "He gives strength to the weary...those who hope in the LORD will renew their strength" (Isaiah 40:28-31 NIV). And David also said in Psalm 23:23, "He refreshes my soul" (NIV).

Sometimes you might be so emotionally weary that you wonder if you *can* take another step. But the psalmist in Psalm 62 went on to say, "Pour out your hearts to him, for God is our refuge" (verse 8 NIV).

Don't hesitate to pour out your heart to God when you struggle to go on. He understands. And Jesus promised what only He can give when He said, "Come to Me, all you who labor and are heavy laden, and I will give you rest" (Matthew 11:28).

God also sends other people to help us through tough times—friends, family, or godly counselors who will not only listen as we share how we feel, but who will also pray with us and on our behalf. The Lord said, "If two of you on earth agree about anything they ask for, it will be done for them by my Father in heaven. For where two or three gather in my name, there am I with them" (Matthew 18:19 NIV). Cling to that promise.

Why not ask a trusted friend, family member, or counselor to pray with you and for you as you seek rest for your weary soul?

Application

* Praise God that He promises soul rest. Thank Him for offering you that rest.

* Ask the Lord what one or two people might be willing to talk and pray with you. Then contact whom He seems to be suggesting.

Day 9

Choose Your Focus

[Let us fix] our eyes on Jesus.
Hebrews 12:2 NIV

Keep your eye on the ball."
"Keep your eye on the prize."
"Keep your eyes on the road."
Where we look and what we focus on affect how we feel and what we do, and today's verse reminds us to focus on Jesus. If we're facing the challenging circumstances of caring for a parent without our eyes fixed on Him, we're forfeiting the strength and rest He provides.

The old hymn "Turn Your Eyes Upon Jesus" says,

> O soul, are you weary and troubled?
> No light in the darkness you see?
> There's light for a look at the Savior,
> And life more abundant and free.
>
> Turn your eyes upon Jesus,
> Look full in His wonderful face,
> And the things of earth will grow strangely dim,
> In the light of His glory and grace.

Always, even in the midst of a difficult season, Jesus offers a life better than any we could have without Him.

First Chronicles 16:11 says, "Look to the Lord and his strength; seek his face always" (NIV). Choose to fix your eyes on Jesus.

Application

* Focus on who Jesus is and the rest and strength He promises.

* As you care for your parent, ask Jesus to help you look to Him for guidance and help.

Day 10

Love

*Faith, hope, and love abide, these three;
but the greatest of these is love.*
1 Corinthians 13:13 ESV

When you were a young child, you might have readily told your mom and dad you loved them. When you were a teen, you might have been more reticent to verbally admit your love for them. As an adult, you might have learned to say "I love you" again—or maybe not. But one thing is sure: A parent who needs your care also needs your love.

Sure, some parent/child relationships are strained—even toxic—and perhaps they have always been. Some won't necessarily change, at least not much. But whether the relationship with your parent is cool or warm, whether it represents love or pain or something in between, do you long for more? Do you long for a more transparent talk with your parent? For a loving touch? For an assurance? Do you wish for the courage to express your love in a way you haven't for years?

Remember what we're told in Ephesians 3:20, that God can "do immeasurably more than all we ask or imagine, according to his power that is at work within us" (NIV). He might just be waiting for you to ask Him to work not only in your heart but in the heart of your parent so He can abundantly bless you both. Even if your parent is no longer able to communicate well or at all, believe that God can work. He can do anything!

Tomorrow we'll talk not just about loving, but about loving "anyway."

Application

* Has this idea struck a chord with you? Do you wish for more from your relationship with your parent? It's never too late to ask God to work.

* Ask the Lord for the courage to do whatever He prompts you to do to show love for your parent, from the smallest act to the scariest step.

Day 11

Love Anyway

Put on then...compassionate hearts, kindness, humility,
meekness, and patience, bearing with one another
and, if one has a complaint against another, forgiving
each other; as the Lord has forgiven you, so you also
must forgive. And above all these put on love, which
binds everything together in perfect harmony.
Colossians 3:12-14 ESV

Yesterday we talked about love and about how we can ask God to work in a relationship with a parent when we would like that relationship to be something more. Today let's talk about the challenge it might be to love your parent when the challenge seems to be at its peak.

First, let's remember again how much God loves *us*. He is personal! He paid *our* price. He reconciled *us* to Himself. He made *us* new and gave *us* new purpose. But what can we give Him in return?

The old hymn "When I Survey the Wondrous Cross" says,

> Were the whole realm of nature mine,
> That were a present far too small;
> Love so amazing, so divine,
> Demands my soul, my life, my all.

No offering we make to God could ever compare to all He's done for us, but Jesus told us what He most wants. In Matthew 22:37-39,

He said the greatest commandment is to "love the Lord your God with all your heart and with all your soul and with all your mind." Then He said, "The second is like it: 'Love your neighbor as yourself'" (NIV).

Even when God allows loving our parent as we love ourselves to be a challenge, we must remember that Jesus was clear: "My command is this: Love each other as I have loved you" (John 15:12). No one's saying it will be easy, but look for ways to love anyway, allowing God to help you and your parent to bear with each other, forgive each other, and "put on love, which binds everything together in perfect harmony."

Achieving harmony might not seem possible—or at least it might seem as though it's a long way off—but God has told us what to do: Love anyway.

Application

* Ask Jesus to help you remember what He's done for you and His commands to love.
* Ask the Lord to help you find ways to love your parent even when it's a challenge.

Day 12

Love Beyond

Let us not love with words or speech but with actions.
1 John 3:18 NIV

In this verse, John is encouraging showing love with action, but sometimes action isn't so easy. Saying "I love you" to a parent who needs care is important, and, of course, actions are involved in caregiving. But some actions can be more challenging because of a caregiver's many demands, the pull of other responsibilities, and time and money limitations. Sometimes the bare minimum seems like all you can do (and sometimes it is).

It's not that you aren't caring for your parent well. James wrote, "Suppose a brother or a sister [or parent] is without clothes and daily food. If one of you says to them, 'Go in peace; keep warm and well fed,' but does nothing about their physical needs, what good is it?" (James 2:15-16 NIV). You're no doubt ensuring that your parent has nutritious food, adequate clothing, and a safe place to live. But sometimes God might prompt you to love beyond, to take an action you'd rather not take.

Your parent might need to see you on a more regular basis. Can you have coffee together every Tuesday morning before you go to work? He might love eating in a restaurant with food that's not exactly your favorite. Can you go there anyway? Even if you hate to shop, that might be what your parent needs you to do with her. Can you take a deep breath and go?

Yes, actions like these can be challenging. But let me encourage you with this: God knows what He's doing. If you feel prompted by His Spirit to love "beyond," follow His lead. You won't regret it. You might even enjoy it!

Application

* Pay attention to hints your parent might give you about what they would like or need; sometimes older people hesitate to ask for what they'd like because they don't want to be a bother.

* Ask the Lord to provide any means necessary to take an action He prompts you to take on behalf of your parent. Sometimes this might mean tapping someone else in your caregiving circle to help.

Day 13

Yes, Your Light Shines

*Let your light shine before others, that they may see
your good deeds and glorify your Father in heaven.*
Matthew 5:16 NIV

In the book of Matthew, Jesus told us that, as Christians, we are light in the world, and that when we serve Him with good deeds, God is glorified.

Am I suggesting you do good? Of course. But if you're lovingly caring for a parent, I know you're already doing good. I'm just encouraging you with a reminder that you're also glorifying God. You're shining!

You know the song.

> This little light of mine,
> I'm gonna let it shine...

Whenever someone sees you smile at your failing dad in his nursing home, they can see God's love. Whenever someone hears you giving a kind word to your mom when she's exhibiting a challenging personality change, they can hear Jesus. Whenever someone sees you honoring your parent by letting him have the last word, you're letting your light shine.

The key is not doing these things only out of love for your parent, but also in the name of Jesus. Colossians 3:17 says, "Whatever you do in word or deed, do all in the name of the Lord Jesus, giving thanks to God the Father through Him."

Whenever caregiving is a struggle, remember this: With your smiles, your kindness, your faithfulness, and the honor you give to your parent, you are glorifying God if you do it all in His name. Your light will indeed shine.

Application

* Ask the Lord to help you remember that your light can still shine even on difficult days if you continue to do good in His name.

* Ask God if He wants you to shine your light in any particular way today, and then ask Him for the strength and courage to do it.

Day 14

Be Ready to Tell

*Always be prepared to give an answer to everyone who
asks you to give the reason for the hope that you have.*
1 Peter 3:15 NIV

When we do what God intends for us to do, He can accomplish more than we could ever ask or think. But what we say is important too. That's why Peter said we need to be ready when anyone asks the reason for the hope they see in us—especially when they watch as we face a situation like the challenge of caregiving.

"Be ready" might sound like yet another demand in a time already full of demands. But consider that being ready with an answer might be both a privilege and a faith-booster.

People need hope. They need to hear about Jesus. They need to hear about the God who can be their "refuge, and strength, an ever-present help in trouble" (Psalm 46:1 NIV). If we don't have a ready answer for those who ask about our hope, we might not only miss an opportunity to point them toward the Lord, but also miss an opportunity to bolster our own faith when we need it most.

Our God is alive! He gave of Himself so that we might live. In a world full of empty religion, in a world full of trouble, we have a powerful hope to cling to—and to share when we can. So when others ask about your hope amid difficult circumstances, consider the possibility that it's both a kindness to them and a powerful faith-booster to simply say, "My hope? I'll tell you. It comes from God."

Application

* If you've never prepared what you'll say if someone asks you why you have such hope, think about it for a few moments now.

* Ask the Lord to give you wisdom in sharing your reason if an opportunity comes your way. First Peter 3:15 also says to give your reason "with gentleness and respect" (NIV).

Day 15

Speak Well

Gracious words are a honeycomb,
sweet to the soul and healing to the bones.
Proverbs 16:24 NIV

The stress of caring for a parent can make speaking graciously with coworkers, neighbors, family, other caregivers—and even to the parent who needs care—a challenge. We can make comments we'll regret, and so can everyone else.

Aging parents can say hurtful things they don't mean—and so can we.

Other caregivers can blurt annoyance when they feel pushed or unappreciated—and so can we.

Family members can express blame if they think their best interests are being shoved aside—and so can we.

Coworkers can make unpleasant remarks about perceived lack of support—and so can we.

Neighbors can complain about the lawn that wasn't mowed or the walk still clogged with snow—and so can we (couldn't someone have stepped up to help?).

Stress is real. It can make us slip up. It can make others slip up. And yet Scripture encourages inviting grace even when life is pressing in:

"Let your conversation be always full of grace" (Colossians 4:6 NIV).

"A soft answer turns away wrath" (Proverbs 15:1 NIV).

"Be kind and compassionate to one another, forgiving each other" (Ephesians 4:32 NIV).

Under stress, these encouragements might not be easy. But prayer can help. The Lord is ready to help us renew our sense of the value in sweet, healing, gracious words. Then we can ask the Holy Spirit to see us through when those words seem most elusive, both to us and to those who surround us.

Application

* Confess to the Lord a time when you realize your conversation lacked gracious words. Then consider apologizing to the people you might have offended. You'll not only feel more at peace for it, but your act of grace might prompt them to a point of grace.

* Forgive and pray for those in your circle whose words have been hurtful to you as you've cared for your parent.

Day 16

Remember Who Knows You

*I am the good shepherd. I know my
own and my own know me.*
John 10:14 ESV

In the body of this book, we talked about the Lord as our Shepherd. In Psalm 23, David famously wrote about how the Lord fulfilled this role for him, and in John 10:14, our verse for today, Jesus reiterated this same role for all who love Him—"I am the good shepherd." He went on to say, "I know my own and my own know me."

Let that sink in. If you know Jesus, Jesus knows you.

Your caregiving journey might feel lonely, but remember who knows you: Jesus. And because He knows you, He offers you comfort—"Let your steadfast love comfort me according to your promise" (Psalm 119:76 ESV).

You might be suffering from heartbreak, but remember who knows you: Jesus. And because He knows you, He offers you healing—"He heals the brokenhearted and binds up their wounds" (Psalm 147:3).

You might not know what to do some days, but remember who knows you: Jesus. And because He knows you, He offers you wisdom—"If any of you lacks wisdom, let him ask God, who gives generously to all without reproach, and it will be given him" (ESV).

You might be discouraged, but remember who knows you: Jesus. And because He knows you, He offers you joy—"The joy of the LORD is your strength" (Nehemiah 8:10).

Isaiah 40:11 says, "He will tend his flock like a shepherd; he will gather the lambs in his arms; he will carry them in his bosom" (ESV). Who better to know you?

Application

* Do you know Jesus? Then Jesus knows you. Rest in that knowledge.
* Whatever challenge you're experiencing today, take it first to Jesus. No one knows you better.

Day 17

Make God a Priority

*Seek first his kingdom and his righteousness, and
all these things will be given to you as well.*
Matthew 6:33 NIV

In today's verse Jesus says to seek His kingdom first and "all these things" will be given to us (in this case referring to food, drink, and clothing). When we look to Him first, our everyday needs will be taken care of, and that includes what needs we have as we care for a parent.

Many caregiving demands will vie for your time and attention. So will all areas of your life. But I encourage you to make God a priority. Lamentations 3:25 says, "The LORD is good to those whose hope is in him, to the one who seeks him" (NIV). I'm not suggesting that seeking God will never be challenging, but here are three relatively easy and practical ways to establish Him as the priority in your life.

Give God the first hour of each day. If you start your day in prayer and reading God's Word—even if that means rising before your parent wakes, doing it before you need to be at their home or the facility where they live or even before you need to be at work or with your family—this is a wonderful (and I'd add, crucial) place to start.

Give God the first day of each week. Hebrews 10:24-25 says, "Let us consider how we may spur one another on toward love and good deeds, not giving up meeting together" (NIV). Church attendance, most often on Sundays, is for the purpose of worshipping God and to our benefit. And whenever you can take time for sabbath, that honors God.

Give God the first dime of each dollar. Caring for your parent might affect your wallet. Yet making God a priority through regular giving honors Him. Proverbs 3:9 says, "Honor the LORD with your possessions, and with the firstfruits of all your increase." And as the saying goes, you can't out-give God.

Application

* ❋ Ask God to help you make Him priority.

* ❋ If you're not already, consider committing the first hour of each day (prayer and Bible reading), the first day of each week (attending church), and the first dime of each dollar (tithing) to God.

Day 18

Let God Do This

The LORD bless you and keep you.
Numbers 6:24

Any season caring for a parent won't last forever. One day your mother or father will leave this earth. Emotions will no doubt be high. But will you be burned out? Bitter? At a loss? The answer, in part, might have to do with how you've allowed God to bless you and keep you during your caregiving journey, with whether you've sought Him and taken refuge in Him.

So on this eighteenth day, here are seven verses from God's Word for you to cling to.

1. Be strong and of good courage; do not be afraid, nor be dismayed, for the LORD your God is with you wherever you go (Joshua 1:9).

2. Fear not, for I am with you; be not dismayed, for I am your God. I will strengthen you, yes, I will help you, I will uphold you with My righteous right hand (Isaiah 41:10).

3. God has not given us a spirit of fear, but of power and of love and of a sound mind (2 Timothy 1:7).

4. I can do all things through Christ who strengthens me (Philippians 4:13).

5. Those who wait on the LORD shall renew their strength; they

shall mount up with wings like eagles; they shall run and not be weary; they shall walk and not faint (Isaiah 40:31).

6. Taste and see that the LORD is good! Blessed is the man who takes refuge in him! (Psalm 34:8 ESV).

7. Trust in the LORD with all your heart, and do not lean on your own understanding. In all your ways acknowledge him, and he will make straight your paths (Proverbs 3:5-6 ESV).

Don't walk this path without the Lord. Let Him bless you and keep you. Seek Him and take refuge in Him.

Application

* Claim one of these verses that applies to you today. Then ask the Lord to renew you with His promise in the verse.

* Thank God for His promises to bless you and keep you as you care for your parent.

Day 19

Running the Race

*Run in such a way as to get the prize...to
get a crown that will last forever.*
1 Corinthians 9:24-25 NIV

Paul says our life of faith is like a race and that we should run in such a way that we'll get the prize at the end—a crown that will last forever. He's talking about being faithful to the Lord throughout our lives.

But the journey of caring for a parent might not always feel like the same race. (It might even feel as though we're stuck in a hamster's wheel.) Trying to keep up with all the demands caregiving makes on us might feel as if we're running a separate race, a race set apart.

But the race of caregiving isn't set apart from the race for the crown God rewards; it's part of the same race. We have the same cheerleader. We have the same running coach. His name is Jesus. Hebrews 12:1-2 says, "Let us run with perseverance the race marked out for us, fixing our eyes on Jesus."

In the New King James Version of the Bible, Hebrews 12:1 uses the word *endurance*: "Let us run with endurance the race that is set before us." Do you need endurance? Ask God for it.

Do you need to know the way? Jesus said, "I am the way" (John 14:6). Keep your eyes on Him.

Just run the race the best you can, relying on God and honoring Him in everything you do, including as you care for your parent. Remember this verse from Day 17? "Seek first his kingdom and his righteousness" (Matthew 6:33 NIV). Do that, and then just run the race.

Application

 * Consider how everything you do for your parent is part of the race you run on this earth toward heaven.

 * Ask God to help you as you run the race in all aspects of your life.

Day 20

Keep the Finish Line in Mind

*I have fought the good fight, I have finished the
race, I have kept the faith. Now there is in store for
me the crown of righteousness, which the Lord, the
righteous Judge, will award to me on that day.*
2 Timothy 4:7-8 NIV

Yesterday we considered how the race we run as caregivers might
not seem the same as the race Paul talks about in 2 Timothy 4:7-8,
which is all about being faithful to the Lord—and yet it is. Now let's
look at the finish line.

Paul often referenced eternity in his writings. As evidenced by his
purpose, priorities, and pursuit, He lived with the end in mind. In the
verses above, he's reflecting over his 30 years of serving the Lord. We
don't know exactly what memories are going through his mind, but we
do know he knows his end is near.

Caring for a parent often prompts us to look back at our lives too.
Knowing that our mother or father's time on earth might soon be coming to an end often causes us to think about our own life coming to an
end. That's not a bad idea.

Paul is about to meet the One for whom he has given his all. He is
about to receive the prize he has lived for all these years (1 Corinthians
9:27; Philippians 3:14). Paul wasn't perfect. No one is. But with Jesus's
sacrifice as his only plea, he knew what was waiting for him. The same
prize is waiting for us. One day we'll be in the presence of the Lord.

Don't let your ultimate goal slip by the wayside as you're plunged into caregiving. I'll say it again: Caring for a parent isn't about only your parent. It's about you too.

Application

* Ask God to help you remember that He has a prize in store for those who honor Him while on this earth.

* Ask the Lord for opportunities to remind your parent of the joy heaven will be for the Christian.

Day 21

About Your Resources

His master replied, "Well done, good and faithful servant!"
Matthew 25:21 NIV

Everyone likes to hear "Well done." Can you imagine standing before the Lord one day and hearing those words? Wow! *That* is a prize worth living for! Certainly, *that* is the prize Paul was living for!

Today's verse is found in what is often called the parable of the talents (Matthew 25:14-30). Jesus is teaching on His second coming, and He uses the example of a man who went on a journey and entrusted three of his servants with money. The first two servants invested the money and gained a return on what they'd been given. Those two servants are the ones who heard, "Well done." The man was not pleased with the third servant because he didn't do anything with what he'd received.

God has given you resources to manage the caregiving situation you're in. Here's a suggestion—not to convict you but to encourage you: Ask God to help you identify those resources and then evaluate how you're doing with them. Are you using some but ignoring others? Have you been blind to some? Are you remembering that God often gives you other people to share the burden of caregiving?

Remember, we can't earn our salvation, and that includes what we do for a parent. Salvation is a gift from God! However, we will stand before Him one day to give an account of our lives on this earth, which could include whether we made every effort to use the resources He intended us to use while caring for a parent. What a prize it will be to know we've given our all in service to the Lord, and specifically to the task and privilege of caregiving He's given us.

Application

* Take up the suggestion above: Ask God to help you identify the resources He's given you and then evaluate how you're doing with them.

* Ask the Lord to help you use well all the resources you have.

Day 22

Faith like Abraham's

*By faith Abraham, when called to go to a place he
would later receive as his inheritance, obeyed and went,
even though he did not know where he was going.*
Hebrews 11:8-10 NIV

A couple of weeks back, we covered what faith is and lived-out faith, using the Israelites at the Red Sea as an example. Now let's look at three individuals from the Bible whose faith was called out in Hebrews 11, starting with Abraham.

When caring for a parent, we rarely know what's going to happen next. Will Dad recover from his fall? Will Mom adjust to assisted living? Looking ahead can even be counterproductive because sometimes we tend to imagine the worst.

Even from the days of old, the saints of God lived with great expectation and faith. Today's passage gives Abraham as an example. As the author of the book of Hebrews tells us, God called Abraham to go, but he didn't know where that was. He just knew he would receive the inheritance God promised if he went, and so he went—by faith. When we believe God's promise of a reward for faithfulness to Him and His leading, we can have that kind of faith too.

Sometimes the Lord even tells us how things will end. For instance, we can look forward to witnessing the day Jesus returns, even though we don't know when that will occur. Jesus promised He would come back, and He will. Perhaps He will give you a promise concerning your parent. If He does, you can trust it will happen.

Once again, the situation you're now in is just a season. But you can live with expectation of things to come. You can believe that what God promises is true, and that belief will lead to faith like Abraham's.

Tomorrow we'll look at the faith of Moses.

Application

* Ask God to help you be mindful of His promises so you'll have faith like Abraham's.

* Ask the Lord to let that mindfulness motivate you to obey what He's calling you to do as you care for your parent.

Day 23

Faith like Moses's

*By faith Moses, when he had grown up, refused to be
known as the son of Pharaoh's daughter. He chose to be
mistreated along with the people of God rather than to
enjoy the fleeting pleasures of sin. He regarded disgrace
for the sake of Christ as of greater value than the treasures
of Egypt, because he was looking ahead to his reward.*
Hebrews 11:24-26 NIV

Moses, too, is an example of someone who was looking ahead to his reward. Today's verses show that he was willing to do the right thing, no matter the cost, because of his great faith.

Just like with Abraham, Moses's expectation of the future motivated his present. This idea is not uncommon. Do any of the examples below sound familiar?

- "I've already picked out my wedding dress and a caterer! I just know my boyfriend will propose soon!"

- "I don't want to commit to that trip because we might have a mortgage on a new house by then."

- "I can make it through this next week of long hours because the week after that I'll be on vacation."

What we expect and hope will happen in the future motivates our *present*. But while proposals, new houses, and vacations can fall through, the Lord's promises will not. Not many things on this earth are certain, but God guarantees what He says, and we can trust in His guarantees, no matter the cost.

Remember when Moses said this to Joshua? "Be strong and courageous...The LORD himself goes before you and will be with you; he will never leave you nor forsake you. Do not be afraid; do not be discouraged" (Deuteronomy 31:7-8 NIV). Moses was able to say that because of the faith he'd developed as God never failed him over many years.

May you build a faith as strong.

Application

* What promises from the Lord do you cling to as you care for your parent?

* Ask God to show you any promises you don't see, and then ask Him to use those promises to increase your faith.

Day 24

Faith like Ruth's

Your people shall be my people, and your God, my God.
Ruth 1:16

Let's switch gears to someone in the Bible who was a caregiver—Ruth, who cared for her widowed mother-in-law, Naomi. Ruth, a widow herself, and Naomi made their way to Naomi's home country, Judah. Ruth had no way to support them when they arrived in Bethlehem, but it was up to her to do it.

Not only was Naomi the older woman, but she was an unhappy woman. She proclaimed to some of the people who greeted her upon her return, "The Almighty has dealt very bitterly with me. I went out full, and the LORD has brought me home again empty" (1:20-21).

Ruth had her hands full.

A wealthy relative of Naomi's, Boaz, not only allowed her to glean in his field so she and Naomi would have food but protected her. She asked him, "Why have I found favor in your eyes, that you should take notice of me?" (2:10). His answer? "It has been fully reported to me, all that you have done for your mother-in-law since the death of your husband, and how you have left your father and your mother and the land of your birth, and have come to a people whom you did not know before. The LORD repay your work, and a full reward be given you by the LORD God of Israel, under whose wings you have come for refuge" (verses 11-12).

Ruth is well known for her loyalty to Naomi. But what about the faith she had that led to both help and reward (she later married Boaz). How do we know she had placed her faith in God even before she arrived? Because when Naomi wanted her to turn back, Ruth said, "Entreat me not to leave you, or to turn back from following after you...your people shall be my people, *and your God, my God*" (1:16).

You might be loyal to your parent who needs care, but also make sure your faith is in the one true God. Have the faith of Ruth.

Application

* Do you see any correlation in your story as a caregiver to Ruth's?

* How might you more fully step out in faith like Ruth did?

Day 25

What to Do with Worry

Do not be anxious about tomorrow, for
tomorrow will be anxious for itself.
Matthew 6:34 ESV

Who among us never worries about tomorrow? And if you're caring for a parent, how easy is it to be anxious about what *might* happen next? *Will she take a tumble down the stairs? Will he cause an accident while driving his car? Will the money hold out? Who will care for her when I'm on vacation? How will I get it all done?* The list of concerns we can worry about is endless.

But that's not how the Lord wants us to live. As you can see in today's verse, He wants us to live each day free of worry about the next day. Easier said than done, right? But either we heed what the Lord tells us or we don't. Jesus asked, "Can any one of you by worrying add a single hour to your life?" (Matthew 6:27 NIV). Of course we can't. Nor can we add a single hour to the life of our parent.

So what can we do instead of worrying? I'm glad you asked. We can trust what's in God's Word!

- Trust in the LORD with all your heart, and do not lean on your own understanding. In all your ways acknowledge him, and he will make straight your paths (Proverbs 3:5-6 ESV).

- Commit your way to the LORD; trust in him, and he will act. (Psalm 37:5 ESV)

- Let not your hearts be troubled. Believe in God; believe also in me (John 14:1 ESV).

- [Cast] all your anxieties on him, because he cares for you (1 Peter 5:7 ESV).

- Do not be anxious about anything, but in everything by prayer and supplication with thanksgiving let your requests be made known to God (Philippians 4:6 ESV).

Application

* Are you in a nearly perpetual state of worry? Reread all the verses above and claim one right now.

* What are you worried about today? Give it to the Lord in prayer.

Day 26

Where Is Your Treasure?

Do not store up for yourselves treasures on earth, where moths and vermin destroy, and where thieves break in and steal.
Matthew 6:19

In this passage (we'll look at verses 20-21 tomorrow), Jesus was encouraging the people to consider what they treasured and where they stored what they treasured. He told them that storing treasure on earth was risky business because treasures stored here are vulnerable to destruction and theft.

When you think about your life, what do you treasure? What are you reaching for? What are your goals? Louie Giglio said, "Follow the trail of your time, your affection, your energy, your money, and your loyalty. At the end of that trail you'll find a throne; and whatever, or whomever, is on that throne is what's of highest value to you. On that throne is what you worship."[1]

Think about that trail in your life. Does what you spend your time, energy, and money on match what you'd say you were reaching for? Now might be an appropriate time to consider your answer to this question, because caring for your parent isn't all about your parent. It's about you too.

In Matthew 19:16-30, Jesus talked with a rich young ruler who wanted to know what he'd have to do to have eternal life—as if he could earn his way. Jesus told him, "If you want to be perfect, go, sell your possessions and give to the poor, and you will have treasure in heaven. Then come, follow me" (verse 21 NIV). But the young man, saddened, turned and went away. Giving up his treasure on earth would be too hard.

Don't be so distracted by caregiving that you don't consider what treasure you're storing and where.

Application

* If you're not sure your time, affection, energy, money, and loyalty reflect storing treasure in heaven, talk to God about that right now.

* Think about how your approach to caregiving might in any way fight against an eternal perspective, which Jesus speaks to next.

Day 27

Storing Your Treasure

Store up for yourselves treasures in heaven, where moths and vermin do not destroy, and where thieves do not break in and steal. For where your treasure is, there your heart will be also.
Matthew 6:20-21 NIV

Now consider verses 20-21 in this passage of Scripture. Jesus is telling us to store treasure in heaven where it cannot be destroyed or stolen. He adds, "For where your treasure is, there your heart will be also." What does all that mean?

First, it means everything we do with an eternal perspective lasts forever. Second, Jesus knows when we're living with an eternal perspective, when we're focusing on what will last, because He knows our hearts. Jeremiah 17:10 says, "I, the LORD, search the heart." He also knows if our hearts are in the wrong place.

How do we store treasure in heaven rather than on earth as we care for a parent? How do we store treasure on earth instead?

The specifics are between the caregiver and God. One caregiver might be distracted by the chance of a promotion with a salary higher than he needs, and he works so many hours that he can't give his best to his father. Perhaps an absorbing hobby takes an extraordinary chunk out of a woman's time—a hobby she could let rest for a while so she can visit her mother more often.

Promotions and hobbies are fine, but one day they will fall away. By understanding a parent, however, by supporting a parent and doing acts of kindness for a parent, a caregiver stores treasure where it can't be destroyed or stolen. That sounds eternal to me.

Remember, caregiving isn't about only your parent. It's about you too.

Application

* Ask God to search your heart and help you see where you're storing treasure.

* How do you think caring for your parent can store treasure in heaven? What specific act will you do for him or her today from an eternal perspective?

Day 28

Awake and Sober

*Now, brothers and sisters, about times and dates we do not
need to write to you, for you know very well that the day of
the Lord will come like a thief in the night. While people
are saying, "Peace and safety," destruction will come on
them suddenly, as labor pains on a pregnant woman, and
they will not escape. But you, brothers and sisters, are not
in darkness so that this day should surprise you like a thief.
You are all children of the light and children of the day. We
do not belong to the night or to the darkness. So then, let
us not be like others, who are asleep, but let us be awake.*

1 Thessalonians 5:1-6 NIV

For these last three days, let's especially focus on your own spiritual
journey. The last thing you want as you care for your parent is to
lose your way spiritually.

We've talked about living with faith and the expectation of what's
to come—even as we don't know what will happen next with a parent.
We've also touched on Christ's second coming, a promise that's guaranteed. And today I want to focus again on His return. We don't know
when that will be, but Jesus might come back to earth in your lifetime.
Do you look forward to that possibility?

Our passage reminds us that the Lord will come "like a thief in the
night" or "as labor pains on a pregnant woman." While those who don't
know the Lord may be caught off guard, we as Christians should not
be surprised. How do you want to be found when He returns? Awake,

living ready for the day, or asleep, not taking His coming seriously? Ready? Or not ready?

Tomorrow we'll consider more about how we want to be found.

Application

* Think about what you're looking forward to. Is the Lord's return one of those things?

* Consider how knowing the Lord could return at any time affects your caregiving.

Day 29

Found Faithful

When the Son of Man comes, will he find faith on the earth?
Luke 18:8 NIV

At the end of our devotion yesterday, I said today we'd consider more about how we'd want to be found when the Lord comes again. Do you want to be found growing in the things of God, giving to the work of God, and going on mission for God—storing your treasure in heaven? Or do you want to be found giving all of your energy and efforts to what will never last—storing your treasure on earth?

It's important that we do daily what we want to be found doing when that day comes. We want to be found faithful.

In today's passage, while explaining the parable of the persistent widow to the disciples and teaching them to pray and not give up, Jesus asks if He will find faith when He returns to earth. Think about that question. If the Lord returns today, will He find faith in your life? Are you actively believing His promises are true? Are you actively believing God can heal, redeem, restore, and save, and that He goes before you, comes behind you, and can work beyond you? Are you actively praying and not giving up?

Those are all challenging questions, but they're certainly worthwhile. Examine your heart. Ask the Lord to examine your heart. Think about how He would find you upon His return.

May we all be found faithful!

Application

 * Ask God's Spirit to continue to work in your life so you
   will be found faithful.

 * Ask the Lord to help you make the most of the opportunities and resources He's given you, not just as you care for a
   parent, but in all aspects of your life.

Day 30

Standing on God's Promise

All flesh is grass,
and all its beauty is like the flower of the field.
The grass withers, the flower fades
when the breath of the LORD blows on it;
surely the people are grass.
The grass withers, the flower fades,
but the word of our God will stand forever.
Isaiah 40:6-8 ESV

Peter ended his second letter saying, "You therefore, beloved, knowing this beforehand..." *This* in that line is referring to what he's said about false teachers in the last days: "Knowing this beforehand, take care that you are not carried away with the error of lawless people and lose your own stability. But grow in the grace and knowledge of our Lord and Savior Jesus Christ. To him be the glory both now and to the day of eternity. Amen" (2 Peter 3:17-18 ESV).

So much will pull at you as you care for your parent! May you determine now that you will value God and His Word above everything else, including false teachings. May you stay mindful of all He has said about what is to come. May you not be "carried away" by other influences, may you continue to "grow in the grace and knowledge of our Lord" and desire His glory "both now and to the day of eternity!"

The Word of the Lord is true, and as the book of Isaiah says, "the word of our God will stand forever" (40:8 ESV). Stand on His promise for an eternity with Him.

Application

 * Praise God that His Word is true and that it stands forever. Pray that He will help you value His promise of eternity with Him above all else.

 * Ask the Lord to be with your parent, your family, and your entire circle of support. But don't neglect to pray for yourself. Don't lose your way. Trust in the Lord, praise Him, and ask for His loving care as you run the race He's set before you.

Beginning a Personal Relationship with Jesus

God Has a Plan for Your Life

He created you, He loves you, and He wants you to live an abundant life.

- Jeremiah 29:11 says, "'I know the plans I have for you,' declares the Lord, 'plans to prosper you and not to harm you, plans to give you hope and a future'" (NIV).

- In John 10:10 Jesus says, "The thief comes only to steal and kill and destroy; I have come that they may have life, and have it to the full" (NIV).

- When we are God's children, He promises to be right with us through anything we face, good or bad. For those who are in Christ, He promises an eternity in heaven with Him someday.

We Have a Sin Problem

Because of our sin, we are separated from God and the good plan He has for us.

- Romans 3:23 says, "All have sinned and fall short of the glory of God" (NIV).

- Romans 6:23 says, "The wages of sin is death, but the gift of God is eternal life in Christ Jesus our Lord" (NIV).

- Our sin separates us from our holy God. The punishment for our sin is death, eternal condemnation apart from Christ. God is just, so our sin cannot be excused; it must be paid for.

God Has Made a Way

While the punishment for our sin is death, God sent Jesus to die in our place.

- John 3:16 says, "God so loved the world that he gave his one and only Son, that whoever believes in him shall not perish but have eternal life" (NIV).

- Romans 5:8 says, "God demonstrates his own love for us in this: While we were still sinners, Christ died for us" (NIV).

- Jesus paid our price so that we could be set free from sin and death!

We Have to Decide

Salvation is a free gift from God, but we must accept it.

- Romans 10:9-10 says, "If you declare with your mouth, 'Jesus is Lord,' and believe in your heart that God raised him from the dead, you will be saved. For it is with your heart that you believe and are justified, and it is with your mouth that you profess your faith and are saved" (NIV).

- "Believe" in the Romans passage is a belief that prompts action. It is belief in who God says He is and in all of who He says He is. Confessing Jesus as Lord means turning from your sin and your own ways of doing things and turning to God and His ways. Finally, we are instructed to confess that belief before others.

Do you want to commit to follow Jesus and to become a Christian? If so, just follow these steps:

1. *Admit* that you are a sinner and that you need a Savior. Ask the Lord to forgive you of your sins.

2. *Believe* that Jesus died for your sins. Believe that He not only died, but that He rose again on the third day. He conquered death so that we may live forever in heaven with Him one day.

3. *Confess* Jesus as Lord of your life. Give Him control from this point forward.

Here is a sample prayer that you can pray to the Lord:

> *Lord, I know I am a sinner and my sin deserves death. Thank You that Jesus died on the cross to pay the price for my sin. Please forgive me of my sin and come into my life. I turn from my sin, give You control, and confess that You are Lord. In Jesus's name, amen.*

If you just prayed that prayer, congratulations! You are now a child of God. The Bible says "everyone who calls on the name of the Lord will be saved" (Romans 10:13) and that heaven is rejoicing over you! Please let us know about your decision. Contact us at www.drgrantethridge.com so we can follow up with you.

It's also important that you find community. You need a support group. I encourage you to find a local church and to identify with other believers. We invite you to connect with us at LibertyLive.Online.

Gather Together

I grew up in church going to a small group. My small group was called Sunday school. Tammy and I met in church, but we got to *know* each other in a small group. It's so important that we attend both. Acts

2:46-47 says, "Continuing daily with one accord in the temple, and breaking bread from house to house, they ate their food with gladness and simplicity of heart, praising God and having favor with all the people. And the Lord added to the church daily those who were being saved." The early church met regularly in worship in the temple (big group!). They also met in houses (small group!). We see this throughout Scripture (Acts 5:42, Romans 16:5, and 1 Corinthians 16:19 are a few examples). The local church involves both big groups and small groups.

Grow Together

Deuteronomy 31:12 says, "Gather the people together, men and women and little ones, and the stranger who is within your gates, that they may hear and that they may learn to fear the LORD your God and carefully observe all the words of this law." Notice how this verse says we are to gather so that we may hear and learn. We help each other grow! *The church dropout rate is five times higher for those who attend worship services only.* You may drop out of church, but it's harder to drop out of community and relationships.

Why is community so important to your spiritual life? God designed us that way. We are made in the image of God. We see relationships in the Trinity. *God wants to use other people to grow us, and He wants to use us to grow other people.* The first commandment is to love the Lord with all your heart, but the second is to love your neighbor as yourself. We need each other. The New Testament is all about the local church. It's a collection of relationships of people who know Jesus personally. *There is no such thing as a solo Christian life.* That's why God gave us the church. The church is not a building; it's people. You were never meant to live life alone. In groups, we find encouragement (Hebrews 10:25), people who will sharpen us (Proverbs 27:17), and people who will help bear our burdens (Galatians 6:2).

People have a lot of excuses for not attending church and a small group. The bottom line, though, is that infrequent church attendance is not God's will for your life. Why would we minimize what Jesus maximized? Jesus loved the church. Jesus died for the church. The centrality of biblical worship is exalting Jesus through the preaching of God's Word. We need the church! I encourage you to commit to regularly attending a weekly worship service. Make God priority by making the church priority. Also, get together with others in a small group and continue spending time in prayer and in His Word.

Endnotes

Chapter 1. You Are Not Alone

1. MetLife, *The MetLife Study of Caregiving Costs to Working Caregivers*, June 2011, p 2, https://www.caregiving.org/wp-content/uploads/2011/06/mmi -caregiving-costs-working-caregivers.pdf.

2. AARP Public Policy Institute and the National Alliance for Caregiving, *Caregiving in the U.S.*, June 2015, p. 15, https://www.aarp.org/content/dam/aarp/ ppi/2015/caregiving-in-the-united-states-2015-report-revised.pdf.

3. Virginia Morris, *How to Care for Aging Parents* (New York, NY: Workman Publishing, 2004), 18.

Chapter 2. Put On Your Oxygen Mask First

1. SmarterEveryDay, "Why You Should Put YOUR MASK On First," video clip. July 22, 2016, http://www.youtube.com/watch?v=kUfF2MTnqAw.

2. Morris, *How to Care for Aging Parents*, 44.

3. MetLife, "The MetLife Study of Caregiving Costs to Working Caregivers," 3.

4. Hugh Delehanty and Elinor Ginzler, *Caring for Your Parents: The Complete Family Guide* (New York and London: Sterling Publishing, 2008), 160.

5. Carolyn P. Hartley and Peter Wong, *The Caregiver's Toolbox* (Lanham, MD: Taylor Trade Publishing, 2015), 10.

6. MetLife, "The MetLife Study of Caregiving Costs to Working Caregivers," 15.

7. Barry J. Jacobs, *The Emotional Survival Guide for Caregivers: Looking After Yourself and Your Family While Helping an Aging Parent* (New York, NY: The Guilford Press, 2006), 14.

8. Morris, *How to Care for Aging Parents*, 44.

Chapter 3. Honor

1. Dictionary.com, s.v. honor.

2. Morris, *How to Care for Aging Parents*, 25.

Chapter 4. Help—Part 1

1. Morris, *How to Care for Aging Parents*, 3.

2. Delehanty and Ginzler, *Caring for Your Parents*, 13.

3. Jane Gross, *A Bittersweet Season: Caring for Our Aging Parents—and Ourselves* (New York, NY: Vintage Books, 2012), 350.

4. Gary Mihoces, "Bill Belichick Compares Patriots' Playoff Preparation To Dwight D. Eisenhower Quote," For The Win, 2015, January 16, http://ftw.usatoday.com/2015/01/bill-belichick-compares-patriots-playoff -preparation-to-dwight-d-eisenhower-quote.

5. Delehanty and Ginzler, *Caring for Your Parents*, 47.

6. AARP, *Caregiving in the U.S. 2015 Report*, 21.

7. Hartley and Wong, *The Caregiver's Toolbox*, 15.

8. AARP, *Caregiving in the U.S. 2015 Report*, 33.

9. AARP, *Caregiving in the U.S. 2015 Report*, 33.

10. Jacobs, *The Emotional Survival Guide for Caregivers*, 64.

11. Jacobs, *The Emotional Survival Guide for Caregivers*, 60.

12. Morris, *How to Care for Aging Parents*, 178.

13. Morris, *How to Care for Aging Parents*, 176.

14. Morris, *How to Care for Aging Parents*, 103.

15. Morris, *How to Care for Aging Parents*, 103.

16. Delehanty and Ginzler, *Caring for Your Parents*, 143.

17. Morris, *How to Care for Aging Parents*, 104.

18. Morris, *How to Care for Aging Parents*, 107.

19. AARP, *Caregiving in the U.S. 2015 Report*, 54.

20. Hartley and Wong, *The Caregiver's Toolbox*, 15.

21. MetLife, "The MetLife Study of Caregiving Costs to Working Caregivers," 12.

22. Hartley and Wong, *The Caregiver's Toolbox*, 63–66.

23. Hartley and Wong, *The Caregiver's Toolbox*, 103.

24. Hartley and Wong, *The Caregiver's Toolbox*, 107.

25. Hartley and Wong, *The Caregiver's Toolbox*, 109.

26. Hartley and Wong, *The Caregiver's Toolbox*, 6.

Chapter 5. Help—Part 2

1. Devi Titus, *The Table Experience* (Oviedo: Higher Life, 2009), 43.

2. Morris, *How to Care for Aging Parents*, 403.

3. Morris, *How to Care for Aging Parents,* 402.

4. Grace Lebow and Barbara Kane, *Coping with Your Difficult Older Parent: A Guide for Stressed-Out Children* (New York, NY: HarperCollins, 1999), 68.

5. Delehanty and Ginzler, *Caring for Your Parents,* 141.

6. Morris, *How to Care for Aging Parents,* 443.

7. Delehanty and Ginzler, *Caring for Your Parents,* 141.

8. Gross, *A Bittersweet Season,* 54.

9. Hartley and Wong, *The Caregiver's Toolbox,* 1.

10. Lebow and Kane, *Coping with Your Difficult Older Parent,* vii.

11. Hartley and Wong, *The Caregiver's Toolbox,* 10.

12. Hartley and Wong, *The Caregiver's Toolbox,* 61.

13. Hartley and Wong, *The Caregiver's Toolbox,* 77.

14. Morris, *How to Care for Aging Parents,* 24.

Chapter 6. Heaven

1. Delehanty and Ginzler, *Caring for Your Parents,* 174.

2. Hartley and Wong, *The Caregiver's Toolbox,* 205.

30 Days of Encouragement

Day 1—Ask God to Work

1. Jonathan Edwards, *Works of Jonathan Edwards,* vol. 1. Christian Classics Ethereal Library, http://www.ccel.org/e/edwards/works1.ix.vi.iii.html.

Day 26—Where Is Your Treasure?

1. Louie Giglio, "Wired for a Life of Worship, Part 1." Worship.com. http://worship.com/2007/03/louie-giglio-wired-for-a-life-of-worship-part-1/.

About the Authors

 **Dr. Grant Ethridge** is the senior pastor of Libertylive.church in Hampton Roads, Virginia. He holds six academic degrees, including a DMin and a DD. He served as president of the National SBC Pastors' Conference, as president of the Arkansas Baptist Convention, as president of the SBC of Virginia, and on many other state and national boards. Liberty continues to be in the Top 100 Fastest Growing / Largest Churches in the US and is a multiethnic, multigenerational, multisite church, with locations in Hampton, Suffolk, Chesapeake, Williamsburg, and Smithfield, Virginia.

Tammy Ethridge is Grant's wife and mom to four adult children. They have one son, Christian, who went to be with the Lord June 4, 1992. Tammy has a BS in elementary education with a minor in missions, and she earned a nursing degree. She has taught in public and private schools and worked for the state department of education.

Grant and Tammy have been married for 34 years, and together they lead marriage and parenting conferences. Their life verse is Jeremiah 29:11. They are G-Daddy and Gigi to eight incredible grandchildren.

To learn more about Harvest House books and
to read sample chapters, visit our website:

www.harvesthousepublishers.com

HARVEST HOUSE PUBLISHERS
EUGENE, OREGON